A Handful of Dominoes

ZONDERVAN HEARTH BOOKS

Available from your Christian Bookseller

A SEBASTIAN THRILLER

A Handful of Dominoes

James L. Johnson

ZONDERVAN
PUBLISHING HOUSE
OF THE ZONDERVAN CORPORATION | GRAND RAPIDS, MICHIGAN 49506

A Handful of Dominoes
Copyright © 1970 by James L. Johnson
All rights reserved. Zondervan Hearth Books Edition 1978
Published by Zondervan Publishing House by special arrangement with
the J.B. Lippincott Company.

Second printing   1979

Printed in the United States of America
ISBN 0-310-37432-4

Library of Congress Catalog Card Number: 78-91676

The song "White Roses of Athens" is reprinted by permission of
Doubleday & Company, Inc., from *The Berlin Wall* by Pierre Galante.

"Be noble! and the nobleness that lies
In other men, sleeping, but never dead,
Will rise in majesty to meet thine own."

—JAMES RUSSELL LOWELL

Contents

Prologue

On the evening of October 12, Willie Gurnt left his job at the Brunsweiler Art Dealer's on Rathausstrasse and walked four blocks to Marx-Engels-Platz and Liebknechtstrasse. When he got there, a light breeze had picked up from the southeast, bringing a hint of rain. He stood there idly, waiting until it was time.

At exactly 8:05 he climbed into the bombed-out ruin behind him, dug into the brick for the small but powerful radio receiver and flicked on the switch. There came that familiar hymn, the rattle of light static. He still waited, watching the sky through the open roof turn to yellows and reds from the neons on Karl-Marx-Allee. He smelled the ruins here, the kind of smell he hated, for it was associated with national decomposition. He had been born with it in his nostrils, had gagged on it during the days of Hitler's madness, and now tried to live with it under Ulbricht. The odor always stuck to him, never washing off, making him feel self-conscious.

At 8:10 he heard the voice come over the receiver, and he turned up the volume just a fraction to make sure he got it, keeping his eyes on the street below for signs of the Vopo radio detection truck. The voice spoke many things there in the dark about the weather, the state of German agriculture; and then came the lines Gurnt was waiting for:

"And when her days to be delivered were fulfilled, behold, there were twins in her womb."

That was it then. Gurnt had memorized that verse from Genesis as ordered, and there could be no mistake about it now. It was "the time of Esau's brother." He waited until the voice signed off and the hum and static were all that remained. He switched the power off, curious now as to why the Vopo truck hadn't already spotted the illegal transmission coming in from the West. At other times they had almost caught him here—but where were they tonight? Deliberately he waited, wanting to be sure. He let his mind shift to the Jacob and Esau thing. He knew who Esau was—the Reverend Kurt Udal. But who was "Jacob"? And he couldn't help but feel some pity for whoever he was. It was not going to be easy on him. And as he crouched there, he grew more and more uneasy— there was no Vopo radio detection truck anywhere in sight. That was not good. Could they be busy with other signals tonight? No. They were perfectionists—a bird couldn't fly low here squawking its protest at the meager pickings without those trucks' knowing.

He finally dropped the radio back down into the box and covered it again with the rubble. He stood up, looking down the long line of Liebknechtstrasse once more to be sure. Nothing. No, it was not going to be easy on "Jacob" now. Something was wrong, something out of balance here. Maybe in the wind that was shifting more to the north and the fine mist that ran before it. The detection truck had allowed the message to come through, perhaps? Why?

He shivered and pulled his coat up close. One thing was sure—it was getting cold in East Berlin.

* 1 *
Shapes in East Berlin

The Office of Internal Affairs for the Deutsche Demo-
kratische Republik in East Berlin was located on Leipziger Strasse, just inside the Berlin Wall. It was a three-
story, gray stone building that had once been the nerve
center for Heinrich Himmler's Gestapo, a boxlike, drab
structure that seemed to carry the weight of the crimes
conjured inside its walls in that nightmarish past. Inside,
the floors were chopped up into little cubicle offices designed to hold mostly file cabinets and few people, the
sign of a totalitarian regime forced to excessive controls.
Here a staff of one hundred kept track of the one and a half
million people in East Berlin: their employment, their
social activities, relatives near and far and particularly
their hot or cold attitudes toward Walter Ulbricht and
Communism.

Every day at noon Margot Schell left her cubicle
marked "Interior Traffic and Control" and walked briskly
down the long corridor, her heels tapping lightly on the
wooden floors turned white with too much scrubbing and
still smelling of ammonia. The hot glare of the fluorescent
lights dangling from the high ceiling had turned this
third-floor "top security" section into a kiln in which
paper, metal and leather cooked together and gave off a
stifling, gagging smell that mixed with the sweat of people

who worked intensely to checkmate any poor, misguided East Berliner who might be entertaining any thoughts of freedom.

She passed the rattling computer section where the new mechanical brains pumped out data on the significance of some citizen's change of living habits and was reminded again that once a week, perhaps even now, her own card was going through that brazen scrutiny. It was probably already digesting her movements of late, her choosing to carry her lunch to the Pariser Platz, to sit there on the park bench on Unter den Linden where she could see the Brandenburg Gate and the Soviet War Memorial on the other side in the Tiergarten. Normally she ate her lunch with the others of her section in the dreary basement cafeteria; but in the last month, she reminded herself as if she were preparing for the computer interrogation, she felt she had to get out of the close, smelly, constricting office cubicle into the brisk autumn air.

She took the stairs down rather than crowd into the single elevator and be pressed almost vulgarly against the wall by the men of other sections, or else be forced to look into someone else's eyes only a few inches from hers that showed the mixed emotions, appreciation for her startling beauty and at the same time suspicion of her as a possible informer. Everybody lived with that here—suspicion. So she bypassed that, and she knew even as she took the steps down that the computer would record that too, and in the end it would put all her strange activities of the past month together and come up with something—maybe harmless as it ought to, but maybe with a line or two that would alert somebody on top to check her out.

She took the fifty cement steps down to the sidewalk and walked briskly to Unter den Linden, which took no more than five minutes. The sun was brilliant after the rain, and the air was sharp and clean, making the drab streets and buildings seem totally out of context. Yet she could only feel detachment from it, for she was a product of a system that had cut the wires that led from her mental awareness to emotional response.

She found her bench in the Pariser Platz empty, for no one took to empty benches here any more; to do so indicated indolence, lack of enterprise for the State. But what was denied the rank and file was open to top government personnel. So she sat down and took the paper bag out of her trench coat, removed the single red apple and bit into it with some relish. She put on her dark glasses against the glare of the sun, but inwardly she wondered if she wasn't trying to put a screen over her observations today, afraid to look at this naked world, afraid to have it look back into her own eyes. She watched the people pass, trying to notice them as human beings, trying to touch something of them that was more than a lifeless card or a computer statistic. But it never worked; she could see them moving past her, tall, short, mostly shabby people, some children—but all of them were unreal, like people on a stage, all of them bent against the unseeing, restraining hand that kept them from laughing, singing, jumping, skipping lest they forget their reason for existence. which was simply every energy for the State. No, she saw them only as a clinical technician who could never reach back out of a system that had taught her well that human beings were nothing more than resources for unrealized goals.

She finished her apple and tossed the core into a rusted ash can nearby. Then she hailed a taxi and rode to Bernauer Strasse to the north of the city, this journey back into time. She knew she was being followed, but it didn't bother her. Everyone in the Ministry was watched; that was part of the price of being in the People's Democracy, more so of being in the upper classified section. She had done nothing to make the computer jump, anyway. Not yet. She probably never would. This phase of her life would pass too. This urge to go back, to stand here now at 12 Bernauer Strasse, was only an attempt to link up her past, to establish the irrelevancy of it with the present.

She took the stairs as before—five times this month—up to the roof of the old building overlooking the western side. And once again she was there on top of that old building to remember how it was seven years ago when she was only nineteen, a member of the blue-shirted Communist Youth, well drilled, well disciplined, hot on new causes, willing to die for Ulbricht, willing to kill others if necessary to further that cause. And she was there again . . . remembering as some far-off dream the touch of her mother's cool kiss on her cheek, the big laugh of her father that died in his throat that night in August, 1961, when the wall went up and sealed him off forever from his business contacts with the West . . . she remembered him trying to sing *"Edelweiss"* as he did during the Nazi power, as if that song would cause the wall to fall down . . . and then that night here on the roof, watching them throw that rope over the side, pleading with them not to do it, warning them as a Communist Youth Worker that this was a criminal act against the State . . . but watching with horror as first her mother went out on the rope, hand over hand, then her father, two people, all she ever had, hanging out there on the flimsy straw of hope . . . and then the shots . . . ten feet from the West and freedom, they died, slipping off the rope and hitting the pavement below with the final sound. . . . Stupid, sentimental, misguided fools, she said again, leaning against the chimney . . . they didn't realize that she had to report what they intended to do. . . . She was faithful to the cause, they knew that . . . yet they went . . . and there were no more soft kisses, no big laugh, no familiar sound of *"Edelweiss."* . . .

She stood there leaning against the chimney, smoking a cigarette slowly, wondering why she bothered to come back like this, as if she had committed the crime and had to return to the site. She walked to the edge of the roof and looked down into the street, then down the long line of the wall, the 26 miles of it, the "petrified worm squirming across Berlin." . . . She knew that wall better than most . . . she had been in on its beginning, had helped perfect it, worked on its plans to make it impenetrable . . . she knew it well, was proud of it; but why, then, should she stand here and look at it and ponder those feelings inside her . . . why mull over it, stare at it and feel such strange ambivalence toward it?

She left it quickly. She half ran down the dusty stairs to the street, and then caught herself. Why run? She had nothing to run from. So she composed herself, put her dark glasses back on and started walking. She wanted to walk all the way to Leipziger Strasse—she could think then. But she took a taxi for want of time, and her mind fastened on Kurt Udal as she rode. Thoughts of the wall came from him. When he kissed her, made love to her in that small room in the rectory that was scattered with elements of the church, candles, hymnbooks and Communion cups, something in all that brought her mother back to her. She didn't love Kurt Udal; it was all for the cause. All the motions she went through, it was all part of the system, to get the man caught further in the web, to loosen him up, to cause him to make a slip, something to put on that card she had on him, something the computer could come up with that said Udal was a double agent. But it was time now. The computer had enough. She wanted it finished with Kurt—no more wet kisses. When he got back from Wittenberg on the Sunday the Reformation Jubilee was to begin, it would be the end of the line for Pastor Kurt Udal, and perhaps that would end her thoughts of 12 Bernauer Strasse for good. . . .

A little more than a mile from Leipziger Strasse beyond Marx-Engels-Platz off Liebknechtstrasse in an open park cleared of ruins, the State Circus was going into its second week of intense determination to get East Berliners into a proper festive mood for the November 7 celebration of the fifty-first anniversary of the Russian Revolution. One hundred and fifty feet above the sprawling circus tent, Otto Kubeksten sat in his basket dangling below the big hydrogen-filled balloon that swayed under the control of the rope anchor. It was a good view from here, and for Otto it was the best part of the day, when he could ride up here, detached from the dismal life he had on the ground, away from the smells and noise of the circus. Here it was sun and blue sky and the lazy floating feeling—and for this moment he could forget the humiliation of the job. For the moment he was alone in the sky while the crowds streamed into the circus grounds below, attracted by the big balloon with the circus clown in the basket who threw peanuts down at them as if they were appetizers for what was inside. And the other smaller balloons around him, the monkeys riding the gondolas with crazy circus hats on their heads and throwing their share of peanuts down too . . . the crowd smiled up at them, but their laughter was hollow, reluctant, squeezed out of the deadness that was in them.

But today the feeling of euphoria did not remain long. It was too late to be up here in the balloons. The balloons should have been grounded in September, but word had come from the top that they should keep the circus going until the weather was impossible. Already the wind tugged at the basket and tipped it dangerously. Why must a circus run so late? Only because Ulbricht wanted East Berliners here to get their blood running for the big Russian troop parade on November 7. But he did not care about that. I am growing old, he thought . . . I will be fifty-eight tomorrow . . . my hair is gray and fuzzy and thin and the bald spot is almost as big as the clown make-up made it. . . . I am one of the finest diamond cutters in Europe, but here I am swinging in a balloon gondola, throwing peanuts to people who couldn't care less. . . .

But it was more than that today . . . he knew when he got down later in the afternoon Borg would call him in and he knew it would happen. He had seen the K.G.B. talking to Borg yesterday.

"It's an order from the top," Borg would explain in his

usual brusque manner that he had put on to cover so many difficult tasks he had these days with the State Circus. "You will have to be replaced in the balloon act . . ."

"Because I am a Jew?" he would ask, but he knew that wasn't the reason, and he knew Borg knew, because the K.G.B. would have told him.

"Who knows?" Borg would say with a shrug as he kept busy writing in his ledgers. "I can give you a job feeding the cats; that is all I can do . . ."

Feed the tigers. Dangerous and dirty work . . . what nobody else wanted, the kind of people the most difficult to hire. How desperate did you have to be to feed tigers? It was a long way down for Otto Kubeksten, he who had cut diamonds for German barons and countesses.

But he knew it would always be this way. Every job that had more money or prestige—riding a balloon wasn't bad; not everybody got to fly 150 feet in the air every day—and the ax would fall. Since the day the wall went up and overshadowed his jewelry shop on Wilhelmstrasse; since the day the refugees fleeing East Berlin by the thousands used his shop as the final jumping-off place through the barbed wire; and the day when the Secret Service caught ten of them hiding in the basement, arrested them and Otto, and took his shop away and sent him to wander in East Berlin, begging for menial tasks. How he had studied the mastery of the balloon, especially the descent! And he got the job because he was a man who applied himself to difficult tasks and mastered them. Now it was done, and he would be fifty-eight tomorrow. . . .

And now he didn't look down at the crowds or wave his hands or drop peanuts . . . not for this moment . . . he was looking eastward, beyond the ruins of East Berlin, beyond Marx-Engels-Platz toward the wall. He could see it beyond the buildings and the haze, the squat *Wachttürmer* standing like pill boxes waiting for some deluded, desperate soul like himself to walk into the trap. He hated the wall, for what it had done to him, for taking away his jewelry shop, his way of life, his reason for existence, for demeaning him to such a low station in life. If he could just crawl under the soft belly of that watchtower, stick a diamond cutter into its vitals, see it collapse with a stagger and smash to the ground in a colossal heap, with dust, timber and armaments flying in all directions—and then escape, with the wings of morning, over the wall to the West, to freedom, to a small shop, to being a man. . . .

But even as he reached up now to pull the valve rope that would send him in a long, swooping ride to the ground, he knew it was useless. Those watchtowers had no soft underbelly. That wall had no hole in it. He had no wings to fly. He was a wandering Jewish diamond cutter, who lived in a dingy apartment and took heart pills to quiet the pains in his chest. And tomorrow he would celebrate his birthday by feeding tigers the smelly meat and taking more heart medicine. And with this contemplation he yanked the valve rope. The 3,000 cubic feet of hydrogen hissed out of the balloon above him, and he shot downward faster than he should have, feeling his stomach jump with it and yelling both in terror and the exhilaration of it. He hit hard, harder than usual, so that the basket split under him, and he was tumbled out into the sawdust. The crowd clapped their hands, as if this were part of the act, and he managed to get up and do a somersault as all clowns did. It was his finale. His hips ached where he had hit the ground, but he wanted to do this last act anyway. He could see Borg waiting for him already, just off the sawdust balloon-launching place, so he took his time, bowing to the crowd; and when the monkeys finally came down, he took all six and danced with them, and the children laughed in genuine delight.

As he finished, they applauded even louder, and though he smiled, he cried, the streaks of tears cutting lines in his red and yellow make-up. The crowd pretended not to notice, for they knew what it was like to smile over the tears. . . .

Christian Dettmann left the Alexanderplatz Church of the Reformation and trotted lightly across the square, down Rathausstrasse, a block from Liebknechtstrasse where he could hear the sounds of the circus and see the balloons hanging over it on their long anchor ropes. He had one hour before attending the altar for the few scabby people who came in to pray in the chancel. He should now be studying the Catechism with the four other altar boys. But Udal was not here this week. He could forget study if he wanted to, and he wanted to. He was tired of the church atmosphere, the sputtering candles burning poor wax, the moth-ball and mold smell of the white altar robes, the stink of old hymnals and the dismal pictures of the Crucifixion everywhere, along with paintings of early church scenes that showed fat men reading endless scrolls.

Instead, he was going to the only place that had any interest for him, the one place that kept him alive in this dreary existence. He crossed Liebknechtstrasse, ignoring the sounds of the circus, and headed directly for the sounds that grew louder as he approached Marx-Engels-Platz. Finally, there they were, where Unter den Linden and Marx-Engels-Platz meet: two big cranes coughing smoke and snorting energy. He ran across the square to the barrier and stood there clutching the rope fence, watching, his lifeless gray eyes growing larger as the red crane in front of him swung its long boom, at the end of which was a long cable holding that ten-ton steel ball. His hands gripped the rope tighter as the ball swung with the boom and smashed into the decayed building, and the dust and brick and dirt shot skyward. It was as if the earth had screamed in pain, he thought.

Let it hurt. Let the earth hurt for a change. Let the steel ball smash into its guts. Let it cry. But for him, he would cheer, as he did on every swinging, deathlike blow, as if he controlled that murderous ball and smashed it into these ruins himself. Let the earth suffer and cough its agony. For he had suffered enough—twelve years isn't much, so said that *Schweinehund*, Udal . . . that "church protector of orphan boys," that "minister of the church" who made his black robes and white collar cover up for his Communist filth, who could mouth the Lord's Prayer one day and beat up Christian or one of the other boys the next. . . .

"Learn the disciplines of pain, Christian," Udal had said. "Pain will teach you to obey, and soon you will learn to accept it as a good teacher and give it as a good master. . . ."

Let the big ball crush Udal in the guts! Some day he, Christian Dettmann, who did not remember anything of his birth or growth or to whom he had belonged, who despised Communists and capitalists and the church, everything and anything designed to enlist him, some day he would run that crane and swing that ball into the Church of the Reformation . . . and he would smash it brick by brick and watch the dust rise like a cloud, spilling out of the broken arteries of that building . . . and see the blood of Udal mixed with those paintings of the Crucifixion and fat men reading scrolls . . . that he would do; as long as life was in him, he would do it. Don't let Udal forget to come back from Wittenberg, he shouted above the sound of the crane; *let him come back!*

On Friedrichstrasse, between the Brandenburg Gate and Potsdamer Platz where the American, British and Soviet sectors once met, is a four-story, sand-blasted brick building that serves as headquarters for the Allied Auxiliary Command for NATO (AACN). For three days four top military men representing the American, British, French and West German forces in NATO had met here to go over the accumulated data Western Intelligence had gathered in the last month. With assignments to the military security section with regard to incidents surrounding the wall, the men worked to piece together anything that might indicate a coming crisis and to take any measures to avoid serious confrontations between East and West.

Major General Bill Kelland of the American forces had coordinated the study, which was a routine pattern that normally occurred once every six weeks. He was still "Wild Bill" to Army Intelligence, a name that had stuck to him since the Korean War, partly because of his red hair and partly because of the long, white, slashing scar tissue that ran from his right ear to his chin, giving him the appearance of wearing only half a beard. But his personality and movement were not in keeping with the name. He was a tall, wiry officer, who hid a gentle spirit and a sharp mind behind a facade of military rigidity and discipline. And tonight, after three days of grueling study, when nothing seemed to emerge from the mountains of reports, he felt uneasy.

Around midnight he went to the roof of the building that faced Potsdamer Platz and offered a good look at the wall. Tonight it was dark, and the shadow of the Brandenburg Gate was like a ghostly shape in the fog. There were a few lights on the East Berlin side, but the view from here was foreboding; there was an atmosphere of perpetual mourning, as if every building were a monument to a once vital German spirit.

"Too bad, isn't it, General?" The voice of Colonel Max Bollweg, the young West German officer, came out of the darkness on the roof, and Kelland turned to see him leaning against a skylight a few feet away, his intense features framed in the half-glow from the light coming up from below.

"What's that, Max?" Kelland said idly, knowing that Bollweg was a very feverish kind of officer, full of vehemence at times about East Berlin and Communism. Sometimes that emotion got in the way of his good mind for intelligence; sometimes it warped his sense of balance about the delicate relationships between East and West—but on the whole Bollweg was a controlled German who usually let his fury fly off the record.

"That everything is so dark over there . . ."

Kelland looked toward the wall, his eyes running unconsciously north and south along the line he visualized. "There used to be a time," Bollweg went on, his German accent slurring the English a little, "when you would sit here on this roof no longer than fifteen minutes and see a flare shoot up over there, which meant somebody had tried to make the wall and had tripped a star shell. . . . Now I sit here for an hour, maybe more," and he gave a deep sigh of futility, "and no sign of anything . . ."

"It is a very tough wall to crack now," Kelland offered, and in a way he wished he could see a star shell pop over there himself.

Bollweg grunted a contradiction. "I wish no disrespect of your views, General." His voice sounded tired now, and it was a strange sound coming from a man who seemed never to be tired or defeated—so much so that Kelland looked at him again, trying to see his face. "It is more now that the Berliners have learned to live with that wall; it is part of them . . . so it is with us in West Berlin. Ulbricht has won, you see . . . he has bent the East Berliners to his will. The wall has finally succeeded in paralyzing them."

"Fewer incidents mean fewer tensions militarily with the Russians," Kelland commented, testing Bollweg on that, all the time trying to dig out the irritating pit in his brain that wouldn't allow him to relax. "Who knows?— maybe we're coming to our senses; maybe Berlin can be reunified and that wall removed."

"Reunification?" Bollweg snapped, and Kelland knew he had struck the nerve that often sent the young officer into a tirade. "And on whose terms do we reunify? Not Bonn's. Ulbricht's! Already he has feelers out; already the Bonn government is talking about accommodation. Who will lose by reunification? West Germans, of course! It will be on Ulbricht's terms. No one has made a deal with Communism in Europe without losing out finally to Russia. We would be another Czechoslovakia . . ."

Kelland had been around this argument many times before. He wasn't sure who was right; as a military man who had seen enough here in Berlin the last seven years in terms of Ulbricht's damnable shootings of East Berliners on the wall, he was inclined to agree with Bollweg. On the other hand, he was also sure that the continuing presence of the wall was creating larger problems: the constant danger of a military blowup, the ultimate plunge into a bloody war that couldn't come out right for anyone.

"So, what do you look for, Max? Another star shell?"

Bollweg sniffed. "Perhaps. Maybe we need something bigger to show up that wall for what it is. We need something to get us to hate that wall again as we did in nineteen sixty-one and sixty-two. . . . It has grown on us, this wall, like a big wart, only now we look at it as if it is a part of our being and not a stinking, deadly tumor as it is. . . . We need our noses shoved into it again. Willie Brandt should see it as we all did seven years ago, with bodies of women and young people bleeding there in the barbed wire . . . then this silly talk of reunification would stop before we get swallowed up in the Warsaw Pact!"

Kelland rubbed the back of his neck, hunting for arguments or perhaps even some kind of intelligent augmentation to the truth of the statement. But he had to think beyond Germany. He was NATO, and his job was to prevent the incidents Bollweg looked for and maintain a tranquillity here.

"Max, I think we had better stop all traffic at the Friedrichstrasse checkpoint for foreigners for ten days," he said then, sure now that his hunch had to be followed.

Bollweg didn't answer immediately, for the change in subject probably left him wondering if Kelland's suggestion was in answer to his plea for an "incident."

"You feel nervous, General?"

"I feel nervous, Max. I don't like all those Soviet divisions coming into East Berlin for the big November seventh celebrations. They never did that before. It's a show of strength, sure, but it wouldn't take much to start something we couldn't finish. It's too quiet—as you say. No star shells . . ." Bollweg didn't reply, so Kelland added,

"Any big groups planning to go over?"

"Only those two busloads of ministers going to Ulbricht's big grandfather display of tolerance, the Reformation Jubilee . . ."

"You checked them out?"

"All of them are clergymen . . . harmless, I suppose."

"All right, let them go. But no tourists—only officials with passes cleared by our office."

"That will mean a lot of annoying delays . . ."

"Let it. And while you're at it, better get more military police patrols on the major checkpoints. I want every suspicious movement reported in to us around the clock. I don't want any West Berliners hanging around the wall for the next two weeks—tourists only. You'll have to do some extra checking and some nasty policing. But do it so nobody will get excited about it or think something's in the wind."

"We haven't done that since the big Russian tie-up of military traffic two years ago," Bollweg reminded him, pursuing Kelland's reasons for this kind of stringency.

"I know," Kelland returned, rubbing the back of his neck more vigorously now, a sign of his irritation that he did not know why he was ordering this action either, and, especially, that he couldn't articulate it for Bollweg. "But I'd rather play it safe right now . . . don't ask me why."

"Of course," Bollweg responded and straightened up from his leaning position against the skylight.

"You'd better inform the others of this," Kelland said. "And tell them we're staying on here for the next two weeks keeping our ear to the ground." And as Max turned to go, Kelland added, "And Max? Remember, we're trying to prevent incidents, not create them. I don't want another eyeball-to-eyeball confrontation with all those Soviet divisions over there—if someone lights the fuse, we could all be reunified in a way we don't want. Do you understand?"

There might have been a smile from Bollweg, but he couldn't be sure in this poor light. "*Jawohl*, Herr General," Bollweg said lightly. He clicked his heels in the old German officer fashion and marched away, his footsteps finally fading down the stairs.

Kelland stayed there a long time, staring into the darkness, almost as if he were trying to see something in the night that would lend credence to his fears. But there wasn't even a star shell. Finally, convinced he might be exaggerating his instincts, he left the roof and went back to the busy intelligence plot room to the almost tranquilizing sound of the teletypes pounding out their steady flow of intelligence data.

He got himself some coffee and sat at the big map table and wondered where the evil might be lurking tonight—that piece of leaven that could swell into a sticky mass of danger overnight. It had to be there—somewhere. And he went back to rubbing the back of his neck.

* 2 *
Up a Tree
in West Berlin

Sebastian caught a taxi in front of the Hilton and told the driver to go to the Siegessäule. It had begun to rain, and the way the drops stuck to the windshield of the cab made him shiver. October ice, clinging to the wipers and grating and scratching an irritating rhythm which sounded like a rat chewing on a wall. This was a European rain, which he had heard described as a cross between liquid and solid, never able to make up its mind, offering no promise either way, dangling it on a sadistic kind of suspense.

He knew the Siegessäule wasn't far from the Hilton. He remembered it from the last time a long time ago when he had visited this 220-foot tower with the gilt figure of the Goddess of Victory on top. Normally it closed early this late in the year, but the man at the Hilton told him that the crowds that had come in for the European Arts Festival had moved the city to keep many of the city attractions open.

But why the Siegessäule? Why would Johnny insist on meeting him there at this hour on a night like this? Maybe it was Johnny Vandermeer's sense of humor—two clergymen paying homage to a pagan deity in a city that had paid its homage in blood. But from what he had heard, Johnny didn't have that old biting sense of humor any more. Back in seminary fifteen years ago, Johnny would drop firecrackers down shaft alleys and put vinegar in the water glass on the chapel pulpit. But the years had put a new thread on Johnny, so it was said, and the grapevine had it that he was spinning on gears built for men of considerably different dimension. And with it a new personality of gravel was emerging.

"Siegessäule," the driver said. He hit the brakes too quickly on the wetness, and the taxi slid to the curb before stopping. He got out and paid, counting out the German marks, wanting to make sure of them. When the cab pulled away, he turned to face the steps leading to the memorial. It was eight o'clock, but already it was dark. There were big street lamps illuminating the square and the tower area, and several floodlights shot straight up to illuminate the golden goddess at the top.

He pulled the collar of his trench coat up around his neck against the rain and mounted the steps, smelling the distinctive odor that went with Berlin, old buildings bleeding their waste of a thousand years. He found the door still open, and the attendant took his money, telling him in a bored voice that doors would close at nine o'clock. He nodded and began the long ascent to the top, following the narrow, circular cement steps, pausing now and then to listen in case anyone else—maybe Johnny—might be following him up. There was no sound except his own breath blowing from the exertion, and he had to smile to himself. Berlin had no particular ghosts for him tonight, and whatever strange intrigue went on in this city, it had no relevance for him right now.

He finally came out on the circular tower at the top, two hundred or so feet off the ground. He moved around the narrow walk between the rail and the wall of the tower, but no one else was here. He glanced down at the wet pavement far below, showing greasy in the street lights. He checked his half-soggy map again, holding it up to see by the inadequate light. Below him and heading straight out in front of him was Strasse des 17 Juni, which led across the barriers to the Brandenburg Gate and the famous Unter den Linden. On either side was the Tiergarten park spreading out before the barbed-wire barriers. He moved back around to the door where he had come up and watched the cars and buses swing around the Platz der Republik, making connections a short distance beyond with Bismarckstrasse and the Kaiserdamm.

It was nice having a geography lesson from this far up, but he felt a foreboding as he stood by the rail watching the cars below grow fewer and fewer as the rain seemed to fall more heavily. Now and then he would look up to study the bright red and yellow lights beyond the wooded areas to what had to be the Kürfurstendamm, the big shopping center of West Berlin.

He glanced at his watch. It was now 8:20. Johnny had set 8:15 as the time. Now he began to wonder, because it was eerie up here in the rain with no one around. He felt exposed, caught on this fragile circular ledge, so far off the ground with nothing over him but the goddess. He reminded himself that he had more going for him than that, surely, but the chill of the light wind and the rain kept pricking him in that place where his instinctive balance mechanism began to tilt the wrong way.

Maybe it was just that he didn't particularly care to meet Johnny Vandermeer at all. Wrong as that attitude was, he really hadn't intended to contact him. To confront him now like this after all those years, jammed together on this narrow ledge, unable to go anywhere, to even properly back up—well, when he and Johnny fought it out in seminary a long time ago, they needed lots of room, two battling, bellowing, snorting young bulls pawing and digging dirt, making passes at each other, hooking with their verbal horns, all in the name of orthodoxy.

It was 8:25 when he heard the steps coming from below, echoing through the tower. Just one pair of feet, he was sure, taking each step with a slow, ponderous deliberation. Johnny Vandermeer was never that way —he took every step with a flying leap, scampering

28

over the stairs as if they were necessary evils.

So he stood with his back to the wall, away from the rail and the door, waiting, counting the steps that never paused, always coming closer, rising up the spiral aerial of that tower like the sounds of a hammer pounding the inside of a rain barrel.

And then the steps were on the cement catwalk. For a long minute nothing happened. And then a voice said, "What is the greatest commandment of all?"

He paused, then added, "To love the Lord thy God with all thy heart, with all thy mind, and all thy soul, and thy neighbor as thyself . . ."

"How is the hero of Central Seminary?"

Sebastian knew then that this had to be Johnny.

Sebastian moved to the rail and looked at the trench-coated figure there, heavier against the dim glow of the sky and the lights bouncing up through the rain from the street below. Heavier, anyway, than he remembered Johnny to be. He gripped the wet hand extended to him, and it held on to his for a long minute. They stood there, each awkwardly waiting for the other to speak, to lend credence to this kind of meeting. And all the time Sebastian kept trying to see the face hidden under the wide-brimmed hat and shut off by the shadows thrown up by the bulk of Johnny's body.

"You've been busy, ol' buddy," Johnny said. He dropped Sebastian's hand, his breathing heavy from the climb, his voice trembling a little. There was no hostility in that voice, no sarcasm, but an unmistakable note of repressed humor.

"A little," Sebastian responded.

"I see *Time* says your exploits around Cuba are setting a pattern for a new era of social and political involvement by the church. I expect that drove your loyal wheels at Central Seminary to the wailing wall; the Very Reverend Raymond Sebastian, the blood of the most famous and orthodox Bible expositor in the U.S. in his veins, dumping all his orthodox baggage like that . . ."

"I didn't dump any, Johnny; I exchanged some," Sebastian defended, and it was like old times, the two of them bristling at the outset, without even the formalities of their meeting settled yet.

"Considering you were the white knight for the cause of preaching the whole truth and nothing but the truth and staying clear of the social gospeling bit," Johnny countered, his words picking up tempo, "I'd say you made a complete switch, wouldn't you?"

Sebastian weighed whether to go on in this vein, knowing how it would end, each of them shouting at each other as only two highly strung competitors could do in any kind of debate. "Johnny, you didn't call me up here just for this," he said lamely.

He saw Johnny turn his head and look down at the street below, studying the cars there for a long time. "No, I didn't. But one thing I wanted to do was to look at you again and see if you are the same hawk-nosed Abe Lincoln who used to put Bible verses in every sponge cake you shoved out of that bakery assembly line."

"So it gives you pleasure," Sebastian murmured, feeling the rain and wind cut into him more now.

"Pleasure?" Johnny snorted. "It means I'm vindicated, that's what! After being branded the Balaam of Central Seminary, it gives me no end of delight to see the great philosophical theologian now running according to the new rule book . . ."

"Not quite that far, Johnny . . . I may be on a new charger these days, but I'm still holding on to the basics. More than you have, I hear." He didn't want to do it this way, as if he were trying to rationalize his own actions of late by calling attention to someone else's flaws. But he had to get it out now, because that's the way Johnny was laying out the string for him. "I hear you've shot just about everything of spirituality down the tube . . . now it's black market, student revolutions, fast and loose with the notorious Berlin *Frauleins* . . ."

Johnny laughed as if all that were irrelevant. Then,

after a pause, his voice became heavier with intent, a note of appeal almost riding his words. "Your time will come, Reverend . . . don't worry. You play it the way you are, as I've had to play it these past few years, and you'll find you've got to do things you never dreamed you'd do for the cause. . . . Nothing but crooked miles here, Mr. White Knight, no straight lines anywhere. . . . I just wanted you to know that for the record." Sebastian waited, glad that it appeared now that he would shift to new subjects, perhaps to the point of this meeting. "I have a job for you," Johnny went on then. "Tailor-made for your new sense of mission."

"I'm already booked to attend the Reformation Jubilee—"

"At the Alexanderplatz Cathedral in East Berlin beginning Sunday, October twenty-ninth," Johnny finished for him. "And you are one of fifty carefully selected theologians from the U.S. Did you ever wonder how you got invited?"

"I did," Sebastian returned, "but now I'm afraid to ask." And he turned to look down where Johnny was looking, seeing a black Opel sedan come around the curve across from the tower and slow to a stop directly opposite. It sat there a minute, and then its lights winked out.

"Well, it was arranged," Johnny went on, keeping his head down, his eyes on that car. "We need you in a Jacob and Esau operation. . . . What comes to your mind when you think of those two Biblical characters?"

"Lots of things . . . a sold birthright . . . Jacob's ladder . . ."

"How about their birth?"

"Twins?"

"Right. Esau is in East Berlin. You are Jacob—a dead ringer. So close, in fact, that I figure mamma couldn't tell the difference. I know it must grate on your sensitivity to the purity of the Biblical record to use those two names for this kind of operation . . . but it was the only way we could set it up without the Soviet intelligence's smelling it out.

Anyway, we want you to ride to the Jubilee as scheduled, but when you get there to step into Esau's shoes. Esau has to get out fast, very fast—this is the only way we can do it. I can't tell you any more because it's classified; all I want to know is if you'll accept."

"Who's we?" Sebastian asked, not liking the way Johnny kept his eyes on that car, and certainly not even comprehending what he was talking about—the whole Jacob and Esau bit.

"Intelligence interest, that's all I can tell you."

"Ours or theirs?"

"Ours, naturally. I haven't slipped the cogs that far."

Sebastian thought about it, sensing the smell of danger coming in strong here now. "You can't expect me to accept like that, just out of the blue—"

"No time to talk any more, ol' buddy," Johnny said shortly then. "We're up a tree here." And he moved back to the alcove door and the stairs. Sebastian followed. Inside the alcove before going down, Johnny hesitated and turned to him. For the first time, Sebastian could get a good look at his face in the light of the dim coach light. He had gone sallow and puffy with too much fat around the mouth and some sagging pouches of skin under the eyes. The face he had remembered that went with Johnny Vandermeer was narrow, well sculptured, alive with the glow and vitality of new causes. It was handsome then, with a slick, well-groomed crop of brown hair, complementing sure brown eyes and carrying a hint of ivy-league breeding that had irresistible appeal. Now that face registered nothing but too little sleep, too much dissipation and too much preoccupation, perhaps, with matters beyond him.

"Look," Johnny said then, his eyes just flicking over Sebastian's face in an almost disinterested gesture, "I can't take you back to the others unless you agree to give this thing a whirl. I know you and I haven't been exactly Bobbsey twins when it comes to theological agreement, but it's important what I'm asking now . . ."

It was not an appeal really. Johnny never did and never would lower himself to that. It was more as if he were spelling out the debt Sebastian owed him, whatever it was, or as if he owed Berlin the same things he gave out in the Negev and Cuba.

"I'll go with you, Johnny, and I'll talk about it," he said. "Beyond that is asking too much of any man."

Johnny looked as though he wanted to argue more, but instead he turned quickly and headed down the stairs, as if mindful suddenly that there wasn't time to talk now. Sebastian followed him, noting how quickly Johnny went, sometimes skipping two steps at a time. His movements were not jerky or uncoordinated as Sebastian might have expected from a man who had put on too much flab; there was nothing wrong with the way he shifted his weight on his toes and kept his body loose and ready. But one thing was showing up; they were heading on a collision course with something or someone—and that car across the square had to be it.

"Stay on my tail," Johnny said to him over his shoulder as they got down to the foyer. The guard was already locking up closets in the circular rotunda in preparation for closing. The single fluorescent tube high in the ceiling illuminated everything in a washed-out daylight. Johnny didn't hesitate at all. He moved out the door and cut quickly to the right, swinging away from the car across the square. As Sebastian followed, he saw the doors of the Opel open, and two men in dark raincoats got out and started across to them.

"Friends of yours?" Sebastian said as he followed Johnny in a half trot down the steps. Johnny didn't answer. They were on a run now across the wet pavement, angling down Strasse des 17 Juni, heading for the protective cover of the bushy Tiergarten. Someone shouted from behind them, a kind of warning, but Johnny didn't stop.

"I hope we're running from the right people!" Sebastian called to Johnny, but then realized it was a foolish attempt here to arrest this flight into the night. They were running down the sidewalk toward the Brandenburg Gate, the bushes crowding on their right. As they ran, Sebastian became aware that they were heading for the barbed-wire barriers. He wanted to call to Johnny, to warn him, for he knew they couldn't go over the barriers without getting shot by the border guards. But Johnny went on, seemingly more impressed by what was behind him than in front.

And then they were up to the red-and-white-striped poles and the wire, and a glance behind showed that the two pursuers weren't slacking off at all. Across to the left was the Soviet War Memorial with the Russian guards doing their sentry steps; a couple of West German police were thirty yards across the street by the barrier and were just beginning to show interest in what Johnny and Sebastian were up to. Johnny just hesitated a minute, glancing quickly around, and then shouted: "Follow me and don't argue about it!" And with this, Johnny vaulted the low fence running next to the Tiergarten shrubs, and Sebastian dutifully followed. Johnny ducked quickly back to the right, plowing through a scrub of lilac bushes, and Sebastian saw the East Berlin border guards coming now—two of them—from his left, farther back in toward the Gate. At the same time, their two pursuers were coming up to the barrier at a full gallop. The lead man tried to break his stride at the barrier, but he went over, landing on the other side just as the border guards came up. The automatic weapons let go, ripping the night open savagely. The man almost flew back over the wire to get out of the line of fire and safely back into the western zone, but this also started a volley of fire from the West German guards, who were aiming at the East Germans, trying to give cover for what they figured was an attempt of East Berliners to make it to the west. In the confusion that followed, Johnny cut back through the shrubs, heading back toward Strasse des 17 Juni. Thirty yards down, they hopped the fence again and ran out to the Platz der Republik. Johnny practically fell in front of a cab to stop it, and they piled into the back seat with the driver staring at them in some fear and anger, using choice German proverbs to comment on the action. Johnny, breathing in agony, half-slouched down in the seat, gave him the address and added: "Fahren Sie schneller!"

After five minutes of driving, Sebastian, still half-lying in the seat, trying to get his wind, said, "If this is Jacob and Esau, you'd better find yourself a better and more willing target."

Johnny laughed shortly, and it was the laugh of a kid playing a game of tag in the park. He likes this, Sebastian thought; he almost enjoys it!

"Ah, this is Berlin, ol' buddy," he chirped, pulling himself erect in the seat. "You can't get the key to the city without that kind of baptism. Anyway, now you know that there are other people very much concerned about what we plan to do in this operation. And we can be sure of one thing . . ."

"What's that?"

"The heat must be on Esau . . . nobody wants him pulled out of the oven until he's done."

Sebastian didn't fully comprehend. "Why should whoever they are pick on you, and how did they know you were up there in the Siegessäule?"

Johnny tried the grin, but it was lost in the puffiness of his face that seemed to have taken on another layer of exhaustion. "Esau and I have met before over here . . . I'm his cover when he comes over, or when he used to be free to come over. Those jolly old Saint Nicks who chased us are Soviet counterintelligence boys who would like very much to get me in a sweat box to see what I know about Esau and how we intend to get him out . . . so they keep me on their radar most of the time; it's as simple as that."

"Where does all this put me?" Sebastian asked finally.

Johnny grunted what was supposed to be a laugh, but it was a cross between humor and disdain for what should be obvious to Sebastian. "Well, in the middle, I guess . . . they don't know who you are, what you really look like, but they know you were there. I think maybe you'll find the tourist bit a little uncomfortable for a while . . ."

That didn't help much. Johnny turned to look at him now with a steady gaze, measuring him, trying to detect his reaction. Sebastian turned his eyes to the front, not wanting right then to show his own doubts, his diffidence about following on with this. He was worried about Johnny's involvement in these things—that he had apparently gotten in so far with interests beyond even his own expansive concept of the ministry. As for himself, he didn't believe he was in any danger for just being in on the episode; what would follow might be something else, though. The way he figured it now, he'd at least give Johnny the time to state the proposition—or the problem. If it didn't fit right, he'd shift back to his tourist role and take in the Jubilee as he had intended to in the first place.

But the Jacob and Esau bit still nagged him, so he said, "By the way, as long as I've been chased around the famous Tiergarten and tested the East Berlin border guards, I ought to at least know who this Esau is, the man I'm supposed to be the double image for."

Johnny weighed that a long minute, perhaps wondering how much he should tell. Then, with his head tilting to one side in that almost coy look which was his way of saying someone had asked a fair question, he said, "The Reverend Kurt Udal, pastor of the Church of the Reformation in Alexanderplatz. That's all I can tell you."

Udal. There was nothing in the name. Maybe the fact that he was a clergyman helped some, though he didn't know how. But it told nothing of the design of the operation. So he sat back and let it die there, pulling his trench coat up closer around him against the chill that came in from somewhere as they roared on into what looked like an endless black hole that was the Berlin night.

* 3 *
The Obtuse Triangle

The address Johnny gave the driver was on Kantstrasse off the Kurfürstendamm. The rain had run off to a drizzle by the time the cab pulled up in front of the place. They got out and Johnny paid the driver. The street was dark, but Sebastian could tell that it was part business and part residential, with rows of delicatessens and bookstores mingled together with the two-story flats. The building they stood in front of was a delicatessen-tavern combination, offering no hand of welcome with its big windows steamed up on the inside and casting a ghostly light.

They went through a side entrance facing the street and up a long flight of wooden stairs that creaked under their weight. It was dark and smelled of cabbage. "It's not the Hilton exactly," Johnny explained with a sniff as they walked up the beaten wooden stairs, "but it's the best a missionary to Germany can do." Sebastian caught the light note of the satirical in Johnny's voice when he said that. When they got to the top, Johnny pressed a button on the door, and they waited, Sebastian conscious of Johnny's bulk in front of him and the smell of rain on his raincoat like that of a freshly opened can of two-in-one oil. After a while a panel opened on the door, and one eye stared out at them.

"*Wer ist das?*" the muffled voice said from within.

"Johnny. I've got Jacob with me."

The bolt was thrown, the door opened, and they were inside.

Sebastian hadn't much time to size up the room, for the door had hardly closed when the room was lit up with a blinding light, freezing both him and Johnny right there by the door. Sebastian lifted his hands against the hot glare, trying to see beyond them to whoever else was in the room.

"Just relax," Johnny said from beside him. "It'll be no more painful than at the local photo studio."

Finally, after a minute of being impaled by that light, a voice said in German, which Sebastian managed to pick up, "Remarkable resemblance . . ."

"He will do," another voice said, more sharply.

"Some work on the nose perhaps."

"He is all right as he is . . . even his own family couldn't tell the difference."

Then, after another long ten seconds or so of silent, hot exposure, the lights winked out and only their orange filaments glowed in the background, leaving the room to the inadequate light from the fireplace and a small lamp on a table to the left by the window. Gradually the room took on shape for Sebastian. It was about 10 by 18 feet, fitted out in simple furnishings. There were two shabby green chairs on a circular orange rug by a fireplace that burned coal and gave off more smoke than heat. A few straight-backed chairs were scattered here and there.

As Sebastian stood adjusting his eyes, a man got up from a chair in front, revealing the white collar and black cloth of the clergy. Sebastian relaxed somewhat at that. He moved forward to take the extended hand. The face was a peculiar ruddy color with a definite orange-pink hue to it—which could be the reflection of the fire, he thought—and ingrained lines across the nose and around the mouth and chin, showing that age had worked too fast there. The hair was white and bushy and wild, as if a comb had never touched it, on what appeared otherwise to be a well-groomed figure. Johnny introduced him as Bishop Hans Richter of the National Lutheran Church of Germany. Sebastian felt the hand in his, and was surprised at the youthful feel of it, contradicting the image of age in that cascade of white hair and the slashing pin lines in his face. And, of course, Sebastian had to ask himself what a bishop of the church was doing here.

"Permit me to apologize," Richter began in halting English, picking each word carefully, squeezing it through the resistance of his German. Now Sebastian could look into his eyes. They were gray-green, sharp, pitted with little flecks of light, partly reflecting the fire, but mostly a combustion of inner energy, he thought. The very bearing of the man belied his age, and there was an aura of inner strength transcending the appearance of external decay. It was like looking at a man whose face had been treated to a splash of acid, leaving those scarlike lines in the skin, but whose eyes remained ever alert, unscathed, compensating for the loss of complexion and seeking to draw attention to themselves away from the premature erosion elsewhere. The face of German history, Sebastian thought, the chariot wheels of the Kaiser and Hitler showing there.

The other man, who had apparently operated the floodlights, now moved out of the shadows toward Sebastian. He was in his early fifties at least, maybe, and dragged his right leg slightly, although it did not seem to hinder him. There was an iron-cross bearing about him, and his handshake was strong. He wore round, steel-rimmed glasses that belonged to a past age of optometry. The eyes behind them were the color of gun metal and as expressionless as marbles. His face was thin, his nose pointed and stuck on his face like a carrot on a snowman's, and his mouth was set in a line of guarded emotion as if he were holding a cough drop on his tongue at all times. A brown, shapeless hat stuck to his head as if it incubated an egg that would eventually hatch the treasure of his brain.

"I am Emil Shattner," he said before Richter or Johnny

could introduce him. "I belong to the Gehlen Bureau."

"Like the CIA," Johnny cut in with the explanation, and took Sebastian's coat. Shattner flicked his eyes at Johnny, a kind of rebuff as if he expected that everyone knew the Gehlen Bureau.

"What of the night then?" he asked Johnny, looking steadily at Sebastian's face with the intensity of one looking for blackheads.

"They chased us into the Tiergarten," Johnny said. "I think they're getting anxious now . . ."

Shattner said, "Ummmm," and moved back to stand with his back to the fireplace. "Sit down, please," he said, and it was more like an order than an invitation. Sebastian took one of the wing chairs; Richter sat in the hard-backed one across from him and moved it well back out of the arc of the firelight as if he deliberately wanted to be in the shadows; and Johnny plopped down on a cushioned stool between them. "We will not take time for formalities," Shattner went on, choosing now to stand with his back to the mantel, his voice sounding like an inspector general's. "I take it, Mr. Sebastian, you have accepted the assignment?"

Sebastian did not reply immediately. He was trying to sort out the ingredients in this atmosphere, trying to fit all the parts together to make an intelligible whole. "I'm still a tourist in Berlin," he said politely, wanting to slow down the momentum of the conversation, cut down the action rushing in on him so he could handle it. "I said I would listen, that's about it."

Shattner looked questioningly at Johnny. "I didn't have time to get him committed," Johnny said, sounding a bit defensive. "Not with Ivan closing in."

"How much have you told him?"

. "About Esau, who he is, the matter of the switch . . . that's all."

Shattner removed a neatly folded handkerchief from his back trouser pocket, unfolded it carefully like a magician about to do his act, and blew his nose into it. With the same care he folded it again as if he had a specimen he wanted to keep for analysis. He replaced it in his pocket, sniffed loudly and took to lifting the tail of his suit coat in quick motions to get the benefit of the meager heat from the fireplace.

"We cannot reveal much more without endangering the operation," he said sharply then, obviously miffed now that he had to spend time on these matters, expecting Sebastian to have accepted already. "Nor do we have time to spell it out and then have you refuse in the end, yes?"

"And I can hardly commit myself without more facts, since as you know I am not in the employ of the Gehlen Bureau," Sebastian countered.

Shattner grunted, and he frowned at Johnny, indicating his irritation at all this. Then, as if he knew he had no choice in the matter, he began a rapid recitation, as if it were straight out of a book. "Udal is a double agent . . . he does legitimate work for us while going through the motions for the K.G.B.—the Soviet Secret Service in East Berlin. We must get Udal out; it is imperative. I can only tell you that he has too much information that the K.G.B. could sweat out of him; that could ruin our operations there. You understand now, yes?"

Sebastian nodded. "But you have much better methods than I for getting him out," he said. "Besides, I am not interested in political chess games."

"He is a priest too," Shattner returned, and then reached inside his coat pocket and pulled out a black-and-white photograph which he handed to Sebastian. "That is Pastor Udal," he said, and his inflection around "Pastor" was not complimentary. Sebastian studied the photo. It was like looking at himself in the mirror. The same hawklike shape to the nose, the wide-spaced eyes, the wide mouth with the full lower lip, the shock of dark, wiry, bushy black hair that stayed short and close to the head. "You see now why Jacob and Esau is a good name for the operation?" Shattner added. "We could try getting

Udal out in our way, but it is too risky. He is being watched too closely. He has freedom to travel in East Germany, but he cannot even come close enough to the wall to see it with a telescope. We must play it this way, then, you taking his place . . ."

Sebastian handed the photograph back. "Since Udal chose to play the espionage bit, I am sure he also planned for the day of reckoning. It is still strictly political, Mr. Shattner."

"He is a churchman like yourself," Johnny cut in. "If you were willing to make a try for those Cubans who had no relationship to spiritual things, then why not Udal?"

"He is a spy," Sebastian insisted, "and my involvement puts me in the same light."

There was silence for a minute. Shattner looked toward Richter now, and Sebastian caught the movement of the Bishop's head from the corner of his eye. "How would you feel if I told you that Udal has the original manuscript of the Pentateuch he wants to bring out?" Shattner came back then, dropping the bomb with such casualness that it didn't get through with full impact on Sebastian immediately, He looked at Johnny, who simply smiled in that anything-is-possible-here look, but to Sebastian it sounded more like a desperate attempt to get him committed.

"There is no original manuscript of the Pentateuch," Sebastian replied.

"We think Mr. Udal has a good claim to it," Richter cut in for the first time, and Sebastian turned to look at him as he leaned forward, elbows on his knees, hands clenched in front of him. Sebastian noticed now that he wore a white shirt under the black coat and vest, for the sleeves stuck out over his wrists. He noticed, too, that Richter had cuff links that didn't match—the one on his right sleeve was a kind of red stone shaped into a musical quarter note, while the one on the left was of plain silver. Odd. The youthful image of the man seemed to jar with the picture of conservative old age. Richter, sensing

Sebastian's look at his mismatching cuffs, straightened quickly and folded his arms as if he had something to hide.

"It is enough for now to say," Shattner picked up the conversation quickly, taking it away from Richter almost rudely, "that Udal's father found the manuscript in Palestine in nineteen forty-four, when he was on an archaeological trip for the University of Bonn. Bishop Richter knew him then, and it was Udal's father who told Richter that one day he would reveal his discovery. When the Russians came in after World War Two, Rolf Udal was swallowed up somewhere on the eastern side—but just two weeks ago we got the message which said: 'The Five Books of Moses are ready.' I called in Bishop Richter, who is sure now that Kurt Udal has the manuscript and is using it to bargain his way out of East Berlin."

Shattner paused now, letting the narrative sink in. He fished for a cigarette in his inside coat pocket, and removed one from a full pack. The striking of the match on the stone fireplace and the flash of the flame made Richter jump in his chair, and one hand went up to ward off the light. A sound of singing came from below at the same time, and Sebastian recognized, *"Du, Du, Du bist mein Herz,"* rising and falling in the uncertainty of the drunken chorus.

"That isn't exactly the most weighty evidence to really prove he has it," Sebastian reminded Shattner.

"Even if it is only a possibility," Richter cut in then, "we must pursue it." His voice ran on a shaky line, pitched high as if a hand were squeezing his throat as he talked. It was obvious his English was not good. "If the manuscript falls into the wrong hands—"

"The point is obvious," Shattner cut back in, and he was frowning now at the way the conversation was going. "We do not have all night here—it is for you, Mr. Sebastian, to settle what you intend to do."

Sebastian looked at Johnny, who simply grinned back as if to say there wasn't much choice where the sacred Bible manuscript was in question. But Sebastian wasn't that much impressed. "So as I get it, then, you plan to get Udal out while I stand in for him," he replied, deciding now to move directly into the real complications of the matter.

"Ummm," Shattner said and removed the cigarette from his mouth with his thumb and forefinger, pinching it from underneath as if he were afraid of it. "He will come back in your place on the bus from the Jubilee."

"And that leaves me in East Berlin," Sebastian countered, watching Shattner carefully now. "You have a way to get me out, I presume?"

Shattner flicked the ashes off his cigarette into the fireplace, a sign of dismissal of these details or a grudging acquiescence to their importance. "That is a project for our people on the other side. A man by the name of Willie Gurnt will arrange it for you. He is a good man, well briefed in this operation."

"If he is so good, why doesn't he get Udal out?"

"I told you—Udal can't get near the wall. But with your papers and the cover of the Jubilee bus, he can."

"But that leaves me over there in the same fix Udal was or is right now. How is this—this Gurnt—going to do any better for me then?"

Shattner didn't reply. He just puffed on his cigarette, his eyes shut off behind those glasses. "What he's trying to tell you, ol' buddy," Johnny cut in, "is that your chances are no better—but he is sure, from what I told him about your exploits around Cuba, that you would be willing to run that risk for Udal, right?"

Sebastian could tell that Johnny was delighting in spelling it out like this, structuring the shape of this to appear like the dilemmas he himself must have had to face in his time here. "There's still the big question of whether I can fool Udal's friends for seven days, his church people and who knows how many others?" he went on, probing further, exploring for the thin places, looking for the impossible fact that would show up the ludicrousness of the attempt.

44

"Before going, you will have less than a week to learn everything about Udal," Shattner said bluntly, as if it were ten years. "Anyway, you will be in the Jubilee all week—no preaching services in the church, no contact with people who really might suspect."

"There's the language, too—"

"Three years of classical German in seminary?" Shattner contradicted with a sniff. "Besides that, I understand you were here in Germany for a year in an exchange program at the seminary in Stuttgart, yes?"

"Five years ago, yes," Sebastian replied lamely, knowing that Shattner had a point.

Nobody said anything for a long time, and then Sebastian said, "I take it Udal and I line up close enough on theology to match?"

Again there was no immediate response, as if he had moved into an area now that was really crucial to all of them. Shattner studied the end of his cigarette carefully. Richter began to scratch the back of his left hand, watching the fingernail marks show up there like so many scribbles of chalk on a blackboard. Only Johnny met his glance, and Sebastian noted there the first storm warnings marring his smug look.

"He's a long way from being a conservative," Johnny said. "You might say that Udal is a freewheeling epicurean who tastes life to the fullest . . . and that is one point where you could blow a hole in the bag . . ."

"Which means what?" Sebastian prodded.

"Which means any resemblance to a clergyman is purely coincidental," Johnny replied.

"It is not easy on clergymen in East Berlin these days," Richter suddenly broke in with that forced pitch in his voice, his hands clutched tightly together in front of him as if speaking were such a chore.

"Let us not get carried away with this," Shattner added quickly. "A man's theological beliefs can't matter that much for seven days."

"No, but the conduct expected of him will," Johnny

insisted. "Udal smokes his pipe, has a sherry before dinner, goes to the theater regularly—"

"What German clergyman does not?" Shattner snapped.

"My friend, Mr. Sebastian, does not," Johnny replied and grinned at Sebastian. "He plays it by the Book, strictly by the Book."

It was plain that Shattner didn't understand. But he said, "You told me it would not be a problem, this theological part. Are you now saying to us, after all this, that he is too holy a man to do this job?"

Again Johnny smiled knowingly at Sebastian and replied, "Not at all. I just wanted him to know the shape of things so he can appreciate what a clergyman has to consider when he takes on a mission of mercy here. So why not tell him about the girl, too, so he gets the complete picture?"

It wasn't as if Johnny were trying to create insurmountable problems so that Sebastian could refuse; rather, it was his way of making sure Sebastian knew it all, making him taste the moral dilemmas, making him see what it cost to get involved.

"Her name is Margot Schell," Shattner went on after a sigh, his voice morose, a sign that he was growing disenchanted with Johnny on issues he figured were irrelevant. "She works for the Office of Internal Affairs. She has been out with Udal maybe now and then less than a month. You will have to careful with her; she is in the security section and is very observant and sensitive to any contradictions in people."

"How careful?" Sebastian demanded. "In what ways do I have to watch myself with her?"

"We do not know what kind of relationship she has with Udal," Shattner added quietly, studying that half-smoked cigarette between his fingers again with that same intensity. "In public it is quite formal . . ."

"But in private, we don't know," Johnny jumped in again, and his eyes were bright with the increasing sense of his inner satisfaction in building the intricacies and complications.

"Do not force the issue, Johnny," Shattner warned.

"We agreed that the girl is the key in the whole operation," Johnny countered.

"He can stay out of the private encounters with the *Fräulein*," Shattner said with finality then, indicating that he wanted this line of talk to stop. "The Jubilee offers him excuse to spend his evenings at the cathedral."

Johnny might have argued further, only to increase the discomfort for Sebastian. Instead, he just looked at Shattner for a long minute, as if the silence were enough of a refutation of that possibility. Then, with his head tilted to one side in that mischievous, boyish look, as if what was said were perhaps fair but certainly inadequate, he shrugged and, with a wink at Sebastian, said, "As long as my ol' buddy knows there are nothing but crooked miles . . . that's all I'm saying."

Nobody said anything more. They were leaving it now to Sebastian finally, after all that. And the silence that followed was the kind that followed people who felt they had said too much. Richter went on scratching the back of his hand, unmindful of what he was doing. Shattner threw his half-inch of remaining cigarette into the fireplace and began hunting for another. Johnny took to gnawing on a hangnail on his right index finger, his eyes, though, staying on Sebastian, intent on noticing any hints of attitude that might indicate his action in the light of all that had been said.

Sebastian weighed it all carefully. He didn't like the way the conversation had run, as if they were holding too much back from him, as if they knew he couldn't do it either but were trying to protect him from that conclusion.

So he let them wait while he decided. He wouldn't do it for Shattner. There was nothing in that cold, impersonal Gestapo character to move him at all. Sebastian was simply another sacrificial lamb that would get Udal out.

Shattner had a job to do, and Sebastian was the means to accomplishing it—nothing more.

And Richter offered little more. There were too many contradictions in the man. Too many double images of youth and age, of fastidiousness and casualness—like those cuff links—and any minister who wore a white shirt under his vestments probably didn't like the feel of a clergy collar on his neck. And even Richter's appeal to save the Pentateuch manuscript—the existence of which Sebastian doubted—sounded more like a plea to save the reputation of the National German Church than Christendom as a whole.

Maybe it was the plight of Kurt Udal that offered a proper rationale for going, then. As much as he disapproved of the freewheeling clergyman who used his cloth as a cover for espionage, still there was a kind of plaintive note hanging over the man caught in a vise of his own making. Udal needed a way out; he was a man in distress. A human being caught on the hook, squirming, wriggling, with no way out unless Sebastian provided it. In a sense, perhaps, Udal was very much like himself, having taken the risks of involvement—and Sebastian couldn't judge him as to why, except that he was now trapped in the backwash.

It was this contemplation of Udal that suddenly brought the real issue into focus. Perhaps he had to go most of all for Johnny Vandermeer. For Johnny was involved too, like Udal. And Sebastian looked at him now in the battered, baggy, brown tweeds, the long brown hair crowding over the white shirt collar, the puffiness and dissipation in the face, the brown eyes trying to maintain those dim lights which faded so quickly behind the glaze of exhaustion. And he knew then that he had to go.

For he was suddenly shaken with the realization that Johnny represented what he himself could become— that this mission of throwing rescue ropes to the sinking innocents, of pouring disinfectant into the sore of man's inhumanity to man, could in the end reduce him to a cynical and spiritually beggardly specimen. And Sebastian realized then that he had to go, though the motive was questionable, if for no other reason than to prove to himself that *he* could run those "crooked miles" and not be bent in the process. For Berlin was suddenly posing that challenge to him here. And in a real sense, maybe that was the other motive for Johnny's bringing him into this. One motive, surely, was that he was a dead ringer for Udal and the best qualified in that sense to do this job; but another was that Johnny wanted him to run those miles here to show what it had cost him to play by the other side's rule book. And Sebastian knew, too, that there was this thing clawing at the inner man that was Johnny Vandermeer. It was there, mostly hidden behind the bold laugh, the offhand, flippant, taunting words that poked fun at Sebastian's "playing it by the Book"—the faint bleating of a man who had gone too far in the dark and was honestly asking if there was really any light for him again.

He got up to walk to the fireplace, where he held his open palms to the flames that gave off no heat. As he heard the singing from below that struck him as a moan straight out of the heart of this tormented city, he wondered just what he would prove finally. He thought of Margot Schell and what her relationship to Udal really was, and what it would demand of him to accomplish this mission. Seven days was a long time to live in another man's shoes. How far did Johnny go that first time he was confronted with the same dilemma? Did he have the right to assume another man's life in order to preserve that life? Was he moving onto slippery ground? Jacob was a good name for him—the great deceiver!

But there wasn't time to check the Bible now for directions as to what to do. He felt Shattner's restlessness a few feet away from him. The night had risen to a crest—he would either have to meet it head-on now or get out of the way.

"All right," he said. "I'll give it a try."

And he thought he saw just a flicker of surprise in those

hard, glassy eyes of Shattner's behind those round lenses, a slight rupture in the steady flow of control. Shattner hadn't really expected him to accept.

"Hallelujah!" Johnny crowed in a resigned tone of voice, signifying his own impatience with the drawn-out minutes Sebastian had taken to decide.

"*Wunderbar!*" Richter chimed in, his voice riding that shaky pitch of his voice, cracking uncertainly in his exuberance.

But there was still no heat in that fireplace, no sense of camaraderie in the room. The singing had stopped below, and the rain was loud on the windows. Somewhere far out across Berlin he heard the nervous wail of a police klaxon—and he suddenly felt very lonely and very tired.

* 4 *

Death Trap

It was decided, after Shattner's insistence, that Johnny's flat was too well known to counterintelligence, that Johnny and Sebastian would move into an old baron's castle in the Charlottenburg district. That same night, around two in the morning, they drove to the place, located on the Spandauer Damm not far from the Olympic Stadium. The castle sat like a medieval fortress on ten acres of close-clipped lawns and tall trees already stripped of their leaves. It had twenty-eight rooms completely done over in modern décor, so Johnny said, and was occupied in the summer months only by a Baron Van Schlesser, a retired munitions manufacturer, who, according to Johnny, had to go to southern France in the fall and winter. Van Schlesser was some distant relative to Shattner.

"It'll take a couple of panzer divisions to get in here," Johnny remarked as they turned in at three that morning in a bedroom as gigantic as the lobby of the Berlin Hilton. Sebastian wondered why he had to share a bedroom with Johnny, but he was sure Shattner wanted it this way, to make sure Sebastian was watched as closely as possible now. "Anyway," Johnny added, after climbing into bed, "sometimes we simple clergymen with our vow of poverty need to be reminded of what we missed—right, ol' buddy?"

Sebastian didn't say anything as Johnny turned out the lights by a swtich on the wall by his bed. Sebastian dropped down on his knees beside the bed for a few minutes. Johnny did not comment on this, but a long time afterward Sebastian heard him chuckle in the darkness. It was the last wry commentary of the day, an odd mixture of sounds, as if the laugh were being throttled somewhere inside his throat.

Sebastian was awakened by a hand shaking him on the shoulder. He opened his eyes to the brilliant glare of the lights in the room. He peered up into a face that had a flat nose, squinting eyes and drooping mouth. "It is time to get up, sir," the man said in precise German, and Sebastian noticed now that he had on a white butler's jacket and was putting a tray down on the side table that had a Silex of coffee and two cups. The clock on the table said 6:30. He didn't understand the reason for getting up so early, but he noticed that Johnny's bed was already empty and that the sound of an electric shaver came from behind a battery of closed doors at the far end of the room.

He and Johnny had their simple Continental breakfast, and immediately Johnny put him to work on the language drill. There were tapes of dialogue to listen to, vocabulary tests, then idioms. But Sebastian had no real problem picking up the language again, so Johnny turned him to what he considered the more important part of the rehearsal—how to take on the likeness of Kurt Udal.

After lunch they went into a projection room and studied films of Udal. "They aren't the best," Johnny confessed, "since most of them were taken by our agents over there from behind all kinds of obstacles. But you'll get an idea of Udal's walk, his gestures, his smile and that kind of thing. . . . You'll look at this footage every day until you become Udal, even to his blood count . . . got it?"

For three hours Sebastian studied the 8,000 feet of

film. He noticed how Udal walked more briskly, head back, shoulders back, as if marching to a military band. The facial resemblance was so very striking that Sebastian had the weird feeling he was watching himself. Udal had nervous movements, which Johnny pointed out during the film—he seemed to be brushing something off either shoulder of his coat or suit or cassock; his smile was quick but often forced. The film then picked up Udal in a restaurant which Johnny identified as the "Imperial," a favorite place for him, and for the first time Margot Schell came into it.

It was obvious why Udal took to her. In the short footage of not more than a minute and a half, when the camera did a close-up of her face, he noticed a face of sharp contrasts—her delicately formed mouth, accentuated by the thin shade of lipstick, could smile beautifully at Udal, but her eyes remained behind a screen of aloofness, of detachment, of boredom. At one time her face glowed like a madonna's; at others it became as lifeless as a marble statue. Her long hair, which Sebastian knew to be a light golden hue that didn't show up in the black-and-white film, seemed to frame her face in innocence, giving her that schoolgirl look of wonder and excitement. Sebastian found himself leaning forward to watch with some fascination as those contrasting images passed across the closely sculptured face until Johnny said, "Steady there, Pastor . . . because of that Little Red Riding Hood, some of Shattner's best agents lie in the cold stone ground."

From the films they went on to listen to tapes of Udal's voice. It was almost the same as Sebastian's, but pitched up just a note or two higher. The sound of the laugh was different, more as if it were all in the throat, coming out like a cough. Johnny told him to try it, and they kept at it for two hours until Sebastian's throat was sore, his head throbbed, and he couldn't focus any more on the distinctions between himself and Udal.

But Johnny wouldn't let up. "Every little slip over

there means a bullet in the brain, ol' buddy!" he warned. "There are people over there—including our pretty *Fräulein*—who are trained to spot the difference in how a man even says his name!"

So it went on till after dinner. That night when Sebastian finally fell exhausted into bed, he sensed the horrible change coming over him, like the Dr. Jekyll and Mr. Hyde bit, a slow, tortuous metamorphosis from Raymond Sebastian to Kurt Udal. Even as he slept, he would jerk awake as the character of Udal cut into his brain.

On Wednesday and Thursday, the tension between Sebastian and Johnny was getting thick enough to choke on. Johnny seemed driven by an obsession to perfect Sebastian into the image of Udal. He became picky over small language mistakes, more and more critical of Sebastian's difficulties in imitating Udal's walk and voice. On Wednesday afternoon, when Sebastian fumbled in a rehearsed mock interrogation with Colonel Chekhov, Johnny knocked a full coffee cup across the room and sat in his chair a long time, his nostrils pinched white with rage. At last he got up slowly and turned his back to Sebastian, jamming his hands deep into his pockets.

Then he turned slowly back toward Sebastian, his eyes boiling over with the black anger that had grabbed him. "I know what that simple mind of yours is thinking," he said quietly, but it was obvious he was forcing control now. "You think you're the big man who has a big God who will make it all come out all right in the end. . . . Well, let me tell you something to put in your notebook, Pastor, better men than you, ten times better—better thinkers, better men at fooling the whole K.G.B.—have tried to do what you're doing. And they had a longer time to practice, sometimes a whole year. But they won't be back to tell about it . . . a wrong knot in a necktie, a laundry mark from West Berlin, even the way a guy wears the crease in his pants, any of that is enough for our Uncle Chekhov to pick out over there and blow your cover sky high! Now you can get your head blown off the first day over there,

but there's the bigger show of getting Udal out first—
have you got it straight, Pastor?"

Sebastian nodded, wanting to retort, but knowing
Johnny was right. "There is just so much the brain can
take in—"

"The brain will take all you tell it to take!" Johnny fired
back. "All you have to tell yourself is that you are not
going to East Berlin on a spiritual retreat! I pray to God it
was that easy, believe me!"

So they went back to the German and the "interroga-
tions." Johnny remained moody and silent after that,
though, as if angry at himself for blowing up.

The hours followed, a blur of night and day—the long,
exhausting language sessions, hours of film on Udal, the
breaking into his sleep of mock visits from Chekhov, the
practicing of Udal's walk and voice. Then the long lists of
names—acquaintances of Udal, their histories—to the
memorizing of nine pages of Udal's family tree, his favorite meals, his seminary life, his theology. And always
there was Margot Schell to study, her background, her
parents' jumping off the building on Bernauer Strasse,
her likes for late evening dining, long walks, music by
Wagner and her intense loyalty to Communism. And
there was time for Willie Gurnt too, his cover man in East
Berlin—his photo showed him to be a man with a placid
face and a long blond hairlock that flopped one pointed
shaft down over his right eye. "The iceman," Johnny said
of him. "Not much blood running in that machine. He
plays the piano too, of all things. He can't read a note of
music, I hear, but he can knock out anything he hears
from Wagner to Rodgers and Hammerstein."

But beyond all that, Sebastian was more concerned
with how relentlessly he was being shaped into Udal. He
could see it every morning when he looked into the
mirror—the smile was getting to be Udal's, the way he
stood so erect, the unconscious habit of brushing at his
shoulders for that invisible dandruff. He could even see
his own more sensitive expression disappear from the

greenish-blue eyes and around the wide mouth, to be replaced by that harder glance of a man whose misanthropic outlook combined with a kind of depravity. And as much as he resisted this change and detested it, he was aware that Johnny was more and more delighted by it—not only because it meant a more successful operation but, important, because Sebastian, in becoming Udal, was becoming like Johnny Vandermeer.

So by Thursday evening when Johnny invited him to one of the towers high in the battlements of the castle, Sebastian was really chafing at what was going on inside him. He waited while Johnny turned on the powerful transmitter, then, at exactly 8:05 on the big clock, announced the weather into the microphone and added: "This is evening vespers. . . . The Scripture for the evening is found in Genesis twenty-seven, verses eighteen through twenty-nine . . ." Then he went on to read the account of Jacob's stealing Esau's birthright. He flicked off the power and leaned back in his chair with his hands locked behind his head, peering up at Sebastian with that maddeningly cocksure smile. Sebastian knew that had been the signal for Willie Gurnt on the other side, probably that the operation was still on.

"How long has that been going on, Johnny?" Sebastian said crisply, trying to shake that feeling of petulance within him and even irritation that Johnny could sit there so relaxed.

"What?" Johnny countered, that ingratiating smile of his still there, just so much lip and tooth, a colic smile, starting where once the fires burned on a different fuel, but now fed only on his nerves and raw tissue.

"How long has it been that you've been in this business of using Scripture to cover for spy plots?"

Johnny still sat there with his hands locked behind his head as though the question were purely academic. "That's what is really eating you, isn't it, ol' buddy?" he said then, and his feet dropped to the floor, and his hands came down from his head to rest on his knees. "You want to know that real bad, don't you, because you'd hate to become like me, right?"

Sebastian didn't want it to come out like that, so he said in an offhand dismissal, "Look, maybe I've come too far, Johnny. I've had enough of Udal, of play-acting. I've got to get off now before I lose whatever I have of Raymond Sebastian. As far as I'm concerned, I'm ready, as ready as I really want to be—"

"Ready?" Johnny pealed the contradiction, and shot out of his chair to walk toward the far window, one hand running through his long hair in a gesture of exasperation. He stopped suddenly and turned to point an accusing finger at Sebastian. "You're shabby, sloppy, tight in the turns—if I turned you loose over there in the shape you're in right now, you'd be wiped off the pavement by Chekhov in an hour! So don't start bucking me now!"

"I am bucking, Johnny," Sebastian insisted, trying to keep his voice controlled, hating the feeling of heat in the room now, "because I don't want to be used here to vindicate your own station in life. You're pushing me into Udal, Johnny, and the more you get me to the point of no return the more satisfied you are."

It wasn't a very good statement of his feelings. But nothing came out right any more; he wasn't sure if it was Udal or Sebastian talking now. Maybe it was nothing more than his own sense of constriction about the operation: the narrow margins of safety, the prospect of total disaster in just a few hours.

Johnny didn't say anything for a long minute. He stood by the window, looking out into the dark night. "Maybe you're right," he said quietly then, and walked back toward Sebastian slowly, hands in his pockets, looking down at his shoes. "Sure, I guess I'm delighting in seeing you fight to hang on to the rule book as I did, but knowing all the time that you have to play this business more by ear than by law—"

"I don't have to and can't play it that way—"

"All right!" and Johnny's feverish eyes came up to snap

their fires at him again. "But you see how it is now!" He waited another long minute, as if debating whether to go on, and then he turned to walk back to the window again, as if he wanted to look somewhere else while he talked. "So where did it all begin? Twelve years ago I came here with a Bible in one hand and a bunch of tracts in the other. . . . I was going to evangelize Berlin. That was when East and West Germans moved freely on both sides of the city. But then came the night in August, nineteen sixty-one, when the wall went up, and suddenly freedom was gone and people weren't coming out of East Berlin; they were trapped, shut off, and I could almost hear their cries of agony . . ."

Johnny walked back to the desk again and stared at the quiet transmitter, seeing it all again. "How do you think I got where I am? You think I stepped down in one easy step? You think I didn't fight too? Every day back in nineteen sixty-one and sixty-two I went out with my Bible and tracts, shutting my eyes to the slaughter of people trying to climb through that barbed wire. But at night I'd see them hanging in the wire, some jerking for an hour before they died. So what did God expect of me? I said to Him a thousand times over. Of course—'To do justly, and to love mercy, and to walk humbly with thy God.' Yes, well, came the day in nineteen sixty-two when I was at the wall and an old, gentle lady named Ida Siekmann tried to jump over from Number Forty-eight Bernauer Strasse—she never made it—ten feet from freedom she was cut down . . ."

And now Johnny simply stared at the floor as if seeing it all again. "And she practically landed at my feet, where I stood with my tracts. And that's when I knew I had better start doing justice before mercy. And that's when I took the job with the Gehlen Bureau getting East Berliners out . . . through sewers, through leaky tunnels, even through the wire . . . and sometimes I got a little busy so I couldn't make the church prayer meetings or vespers, you know what I mean?" and Johnny's eyes came up to fix on Sebastian again, and his nostrils were white and pinched. "But it's been my Gethsemane, ol' buddy, and it's been worth it all just to give a man, a boy or girl a chance at life." He paused again, and the room was almost stifling for Sebastian. "So don't stand there and tell me you resent becoming Johnny Vandermeer or Udal! It's a sacred order, buddy, and you have a lot of sweating to do yet before you qualify, got it?"

And Johnny laughed then as if it were an appeal for understanding. And neither of them spoke for a long time. Whatever Sebastian had in mind in opening the conversation had gone now, dissolved in the backwash of Johnny's self-exposure. If anything, he felt confused, even as Johnny now seemed embarrassed, as if he had said more than he intended. For Sebastian, the experience was like the shattering of an image. Johnny—that brash, cocky, debonair, sanguine character—was suddenly closer to the true humility of a man of God than Sebastian himself had ever been. It was almost painful to have to adjust his mental focus to a side he'd never expected to see.

Their thoughts were finally disturbed by the sound of the Oriental gong reverberating through the castle chambers, announcing that someone was at the door. It came as a kind of relief for Johnny who, without a word, breezed by Sebastian and out the door. A minute later Sebastian followed, still fingering the pieces of Johnny's appeal in his mind.

When he got down to the main floor, he found Shattner waiting. He was standing by a long table in the receiving hall, smoking a cigarette as usual. He watched Sebastian closely as he walked in, then said to Johnny, "He begins to look like Udal more and more . . . that is good, very good." Johnny said nothing. They sat down at the long table, and Shattner pulled out a small bag and began to remove the instruments. He plugged into a wall socket the cord of a six-inch object; it had a blunt needle at the end.

"Roll up your sleeve, Mr. Sebastian," he said simply, again commanding, not inviting.

"What for?"

Shattner sniffed his disdain of the question. "We must tattoo some numbers on your upper arm below the armpit. . . . Udal was once registered as a boy for Buchenwald concentration camp. His father was able to intercede for him and the whole family by taking the job at the university. You must have that number on you, for that is what the K.G.B. will look for first . . ."

"You're making it permanent?" asked Sebastian, certain he did not like this at all, as Shattner began his work.

"In time it will rub off . . . but we must make it look as if it has been there for years. It won't take long."

It took a good twenty minutes. Could anything more be needed to make him the carbon copy of Udal? Afterward, Shattner packed his things and Sebastian asked, "By the way, where is Bishop Richter these days?"

Shattner went on stuffing his bag, not answering, savoring it as he did every question put to him. Then he straightened up and his eyes fixed their glassy stare at Sebastian as though he'd been asked his bank balance. "Ummm," he began, as if rolling the cough drop in his mouth to one side so he could talk. "Bishop Richter is this week at the Kaiser Wilhelm Church . . . he will help dedicate the new carillon they are installing tomorrow. Now, then, gentlemen, *auf Wiedersehen!*"

Sebastian sat at the table a long time afterward, and Johnny did not seem particularly anxious to move. "How do you figure Richter?" he asked Johnny finally.

"What do you mean?" and Johnny began to pick up his notes slowly as if he suddenly wanted to call it quits.

"I mean, how does he strike you? I get the feeling he's about as easy to know as a piece of fog."

Johnny didn't say anything. He seemed preoccupied suddenly, out of sorts. Then, scooping up the last of his papers into a briefcase, he headed out of the room, tossing the answer over his shoulder, "That's the Germans for you, I guess. . . . By the way, turn out the lights before you turn in, will you? I'm going to be tied up in the drawing room most of the night. Better get some sleep. You'll need it."

Sebastian went to bed and sat reading over the notes on Udal's history. He couldn't stop thinking of Johnny. He was disturbed, prowling over this thing. He knew that for Johnny to lay himself bare as he had in the tower, to offer almost an apology for what he was doing as a minister in Berlin, meant he had to be hurting somewhere—that the water had risen and was threatening to engulf him. Sebastian didn't particularly like that ingredient to come into the operation this late; anything out of balance now magnified the risks, injecting a sort of metal fatigue into the whole structure.

At midnight he dropped off to sleep. He woke with a start. He noticed it was two o'clock. Johnny's bed hadn't been slept in. And then he heard the low drone of voices downstairs, coming more directly, it seemed, from the drawing room below. He sat up listening, trying to pick out Johnny's voice. Finally he lay back when the sounds died again, staring a long time at the ceiling, wondering—and he knew it was there to stay now, that eerie feeling that came over a man who was groping his way in a dark room, never sure what he would hit next. But he had been this way before, he told himself—so he pushed his nagging doubts aside, wanting only to get the sleep he so desperately needed. He reached over and turned out the light.

On Friday Johnny put him through the final and toughest test. At eleven o'clock that morning a Mr. Dorf Frantzel, a close cousin of Udal's who had escaped from East Berlin two years ago, was to come for lunch. He knew nothing of Sebastian's presence. Johnny was nervous about it. "If he picks out the small differences right away, we're sunk," he told Sebastian.

At eleven the gong echoed throughout the castle. Rudy, the butler, let the man in. Sebastian stayed in the receiving hall in front of the fireplace that gave off a pleasant, crackling heat. He stood with his hands behind his back, as he had seen Udal do in the film, his shoulders at military stiffness, his head cocked to the right, that small, nervous smile turned on. Johnny came around the corner with Frantzel. He was a short, fat man in his late forties maybe, dressed in a black suit with a massive gold watch chain hanging across his ponderous, jiggling belly. He was holding a cup of coffee in his left hand, balancing it with the expertness of a waiter. When he came around the settee, he was talking to Johnny, and he glanced up politely as he approached Sebastian. In that instant he froze, stopping no more than ten feet away. His fat face, rouged with high blood pressure, went pale; his lifeless gray eyes widened; and the cup fell out of his hand to hit the rug with a slight thumping sound.

"*Mein Gott!*" he exclaimed, his hand flying up to his mouth that was still wet from the coffee. "Kurt!" Then he threw a quick accusing glance at Johnny. "I did not know Kurt was here, Herr Vandermeer!"

Johnny went through some explanations but added that the man he was looking at was not Udal but Raymond Sebastian, visiting from the States. "A guest in West Berlin for a couple of weeks," he said.

"When and how did you get out?" Frantzel cut in, ignoring Johnny's explanations. By now he was visibly trembling, and Sebastian shot a warning glance at Johnny. It took time, but finally Frantzel reluctantly accepted Johnny's word that Sebastian was not Udal. "The shock of this," he added. "You will forgive me, Herr Vandermeer—perhaps you will not think me unkind if I do not stay to lunch?"

Johnny led him to the door, assuring him it was all right and apologizing for not preparing Frantzel better. At the door Frantzel paused to give Sebastian one more long look. "It is hard not to believe it is not you, Kurt," and then he went out, shaking his head.

Johnny came back into the room and gave Sebastian a

quick grin, a salute to success. "If you fooled Frantzel, you'll give them over on the other side a fair whirl for their money," he said shortly. "So let's wind this up with the last few strings we've got left, shall we?"

They went over the street guide of East Berlin during lunch, Johnny pointing out the six crossing points and even the train routes by either the U-Bahn or S-Bahn. In the late afternoon they went over the structure of "Ulbricht's Wonder," the hated wall now made totally impenetrable by new traps and other safety measures. Johnny drew it out for him. First the animal fence, five feet high. Then the alarm fence that, when touched, sent a signal to the watchtower and the armored car; the dog run, the trip wires that set off the flares, the tank trap. If a man was lucky to get that far, there were ten yards of grass that hid spikes sticking up, and beyond that the last ten yards of mines before the wall. The final hurdle was the fifteen-foot wall with the eight-inch pipe on top, too thick for a hand hold.

"In other words, ol' buddy, forget the wall," Johnny concluded. "Your only hope is the checkpoints—and Willie Gurnt probably has that doped out."

There was nothing more to say. They went over a few details on Udal, and they had Rudy serve them dinner early. Johnny said little during the meal. He seemed moody. Finally, pushing the dishes aside, he said, "You're ready as you'll ever be now. All you have to worry about is Margot Schell. You got any questions?"

Sebastian wanted to talk some more, about anything, just to know more about Johnny. But Johnny wasn't going to linger, even though it seemed as if he found it hard now too to break it up. He stood up, stared down at his plate a minute as if trying to remember something, and then waved his hand in dismissal and walked out of the room.

Sebastian went to bed at the usual time and woke up to the sound of voices again from the drawing room. They rose loudly once, and he heard what had to be Johnny's voice shouting, "But he's already done more than you can expect . . ." And then someone else cut in on him, and the voices were but a mumble again. Sebastian wondered if he should check on it; but he was afraid of hearing too much, seeing too much and being weighted down with more complications. Instead, he sank back on the pillows and forced himself back to sleep.

On Saturday he saw little of Johnny. He had gone out after breakfast, Rudy said, and would be back in the afternoon. But by four he hadn't shown up. By eight Sebastian was getting worried and thought of calling Shattner. But Shattner had said no calls to him at the Gehlen Bureau. Finally, at nine, he asked Rudy if he knew where Johnny might be. Rudy scowled in concentration, looking like a disgruntled bulldog.

"Kaiser Wilhelm Church," he said finally.

"Why there?"

"Richter—he was here last night . . . they talked long into the morning. Shattner too. I think he is there now, yes?"

Sebastian finally persuaded Rudy to call a cab and check at the church, even though the big man didn't think there was cause for worry. After he had gone, Sebastian paced up and down the long receiving room, sensing in the shadows from the empty suits of armor hanging out from the walls the silent witnesses of people long gone who had faced their crises at one time.

It was about twenty minutes after Rudy left that he heard the sound at the big oak door. He wasn't sure at first, but when he walked up to it cautiously, he saw the big brass knob turning slowly. Quickly he jerked it open a fraction, and Johnny leaned in, shoving his one trench-coated arm inside, his hand trying to grab something. Sebastian swung the big door wider, and Johnny fell forward. Sebastian caught him before he hit the floor, and he saw immediately that Johnny was hurt—very badly. There was a lot of blood on the front of his trench coat, and a mass of red on his shirt. His face was drawn, almost ashen; his dark eyes were bigger now, and he tried moving his mouth to say something, his hand gripping Sebastian's shirt.

"I'll get a doctor, Johnny," Sebastian said, trying to lay him down there on the rug inside the door.

"N—no," Johnny croaked, and the word came out on the end of a long, liquid-sounding gasp. Sebastian eased him down on the rug, and now he noticed that Johnny's breathing was shallow and rapid, and his eyes were taking on a glaze. He tried to say something else, but instead lifted his hand and opened the fist slowly. Sebastian took the balled-up piece of blue-lined paper from it, put it into his shirt pocket and tried to get his mind working to take some action to head off the roaring sound of death in the room. But then another of those long, trembling sighs came from Johnny, and he reached up to grab Sebastian by the lapels of his shirt front. Only a faint smile crossed his puffy mouth, and then the fixed stare came into those eyes, and his body went limp there on the rug. The room fell quiet, and only the breeze that came in from the door rustled through the room, filling the cavernous castle with a chill.

"Dear God," Sebastian said in a whisper, staring down at the sagging flesh of Johnny's face, seeing in death now the boyish features he once knew in seminary. Then he got up quickly, moved suddenly by the enormity of this thing. He closed the door, then got on the phone, dialing Shattner's number. The voice on the other end was as coldly detached as ever.

"This is Sebastian. . . . Johnny's dead. You'd better come over."

"Five minutes," Shattner said crisply and hung up.

Sebastian stood against the wall, looking down at the body, fighting off the numbness that came with the shock, wishing now that he had taken time to reach Johnny, to understand him better—maybe tell him he didn't have to feel bad about what he was doing here. But then good thoughts of a man always seemed to come too late.

Shattner was there in ten minutes. He didn't say a word to Sebastian. He bent over, examined Johnny's wounds, then stood up, resting his hands on his hips. "He was not supposed to go out," he said shortly. "Where did he go?"

"I don't know . . . Rudy thought Kaiser Wilhelm Church. To see Richter."

Shattner shook his head. "Has to be the work of the Soviet intelligence. They caught up to him at last."

Just then Rudy came in the front door and meant to say something to Sebastian. Instead, he stood there looking at the body, a forlorn look crossing his homely face. Then he turned his back to Johnny, stiffly facing the door.

"Johnny once got his grandmother out of East Berlin," Shattner said, jerking his head toward Rudy. What difference did it make now? Sebastian thought. "I suppose you feel that the operation is useless now," Shattner added, "without Johnny?" That showed where Shattner's interests were: the Jubilee tomorrow, Udal, Jacob and Esau.

"Why shoot him," Sebastian demanded, ignoring Shattner's question, "like some animal running in the streets? Why?"

Shattner sniffed. "You don't ask questions like that here," he said coldly. He began hunting for a cigarette, found one, put it into his mouth. Then he tipped his hat back on his forehead, revealing a few strands of wet, gray-black hair against the pink of his baldness. It was almost indecent seeing his head bared even that much. "Johnny took his chances like all of us. This is not child's play. This operation is big; we know it, Ivan knows it. When you play big, you take big chances, yes?" He struck a match on the floor next to Johnny's body and lit his cigarette.

"Who will see to him now?" Sebastian asked, anxious that Johnny at least get a decent burial.

Shattner shrugged. "He had no family at home, so he told me. I will be glad to take care of him."

"Bury him by the wall," Sebastian added. Then he looked up at Shattner, who was peering at him steadily, his eyes hidden behind the glint of those glasses. "Can you do that? He talked about Ida—I don't know exactly—"

"Siekmann?"

"Yes. Could he be buried somewhere near there like those others who died trying to get over the wall? Can you do it?"

Shattner thought about it a minute, sucking on his cigarette, blowing smoke across Johnny in a gesture of dismissal. "I can do it. . . . It will take some fixing, but I can do it."

"Thank you," Sebastian said and turned to walk away.

"Mr. Sebastian," Shattner's voice reached out to him, controlling him on that authoritative leash. "We must transmit the last message to Gurnt tonight. You will still go?"

Sebastian paused, halfway turning to look back at Johnny. "He died for something," he said finally. "I owe it to him to find out what for."

"Good. Then you will have to be at the check-in for the buses by three tomorrow afternoon. You should go back to the Hilton tonight and leave from there."

"Very well. I'll get Johnny's things."

He went to his room and began gathering up his own few articles and what Johnny had left. There wasn't much. A comb, a key chain, a small pocket New Testament, the larger complete Bible from which he read the Genesis account. That's all there was—except a clipping from a Chicago newspaper and *Time* magazine's account of Sebastian's escapades around Cuba. And looking at it, Sebastian felt ashamed of his efforts there compared to what Johnny must have done these years in Berlin. And not one headline of his own, not even a decent line on him in the *Central Seminary Bulletin*.

He moved to put the clipping in his shirt pocket and then remembered the piece of paper Johnny had given him before he died. He dug it out and read: Genesis 27:41.

He opened the Bible to the chapter and verse and read: "And Esau said in his heart; then will I slay my brother Jacob."

There it was, what Johnny must have been on his way to tell him—perhaps dragging himself the last painful miles or yards to deliver it. Something he had found out. Was that what he was arguing about in the drawing room with Shattner and Richter last night? Johnny, what are you trying to say? Where does Richter fit in? Even Shattner? Do they know? Dear God, is Udal waiting over there to kill me?

He debated whether to share it with Shattner; but then he figured this was something Johnny had stayed alive long enough to deliver personally. So he put it back into his shirt pocket. When he got back to the receiving room, Shattner was waiting. Rudy had already gone. They waited until the ambulance arrived and picked up Johnny. Then Shattner drove him to the Hilton. They said nothing to each other during the drive.

At the hotel, Shattner reached out his hand before Sebastian got out and said, "Good luck." Sebastian took the cold chunk of flesh in his hand, dropping it quickly, not feeling any comradeship with Shattner at all in this.

"I'll leave the burial to you," he said, and got out and stood on the sidewalk as Shattner drove away.

Music was coming from the Hilton, gay, convivial, telling of a slice of humanity concerned only with ways to kill their boredom. Down the street the Siegessäule lights were a dim, bony arm jabbing into the belly of the shrouded sky; beyond was the Brandenburg Gate. Tomorrow he would be in that other nation. Tonight he would be alone with his mourning and confusion. Tomorrow night this time he would be Kurt Udal. And he felt a shiver as the light wind touched his cheek. It was like the wind that had followed Johnny into the castle—carrying no fragrance, no promise of sun or warmth. It was straight out of hell. And no man should stand in it, he said to himself, as he walked toward the hotel and the music. . . . But I shall run before it tomorrow . . . all those long, lonely crooked miles.

* 5 *
The Pinch
of Esau's Shoes

The three buses carrying ninety-six clergymen from all over the world crossed through the Friedrichstrasse Checkpoint for foreigners at four o'clock on Sunday afternoon. The sun was bright but filtered through a chill atmosphere so that there was a brittleness to the world, making everything look as fragile as crystal. It was nearly six o'clock before the barrier was lifted and the buses were cleared to proceed. It was getting dark by then, but as they crossed over the Zimmerstrasse tram tracks into the Communist world, Sebastian felt the difference. Whether it was psychological or not, it was different. Even the laughing, boisterous, good-natured sounds of the others on the bus died down; it was like viewing a body, paying respects for the life it once had. Something in the buildings perhaps, the way they seemed to bunch together in their dismal cloaks of dirty gray or black— gloomy sentinels protecting the good memories they might be harboring against the encroachment of whatever was here now. Even the lights glowed at half power, fighting the stultifying darkness, making an attempt to be cheerful. But it was all hopeless.

They turned right on Unter den Linden, drove by the old Bismarck Chancellery, then around to Karl-Marx-Allee. It was a long detour to Alexanderplatz, but their young East German guide wanted them to see this display case of Ulbricht's new economic order. In the darkness it didn't come off too well, so the guide ordered the bus on into Alexanderplatz without much further comment.

As they approached the cathedral, Sebastian began to tense up. His mind came to full attention. All the rehearsing with Johnny of these opening moves had to pay off now. The buses swung into the circular cobblestone drive in front of the cathedral that hung out against the night with its abutments and towers. Sebastian followed the others off the bus and walked casually up the long walk to the double doors, noting that there were many Volkspolizei around and even a few Russian military policemen. But as he came to the doors, he noticed no uniforms there. That was going to make it a little easier anyway.

He stepped inside, following several other American clergymen who carried the familiar Pan Am flight bags over their shoulders. Noticing the stairs going down to the right, he made the turn in a move that was, he hoped, not jerky or hurried. He was not more than five steps down when a voice in English called to him, "I think we go straight ahead, brother!"

He glanced up quickly to see a tall, lanky clergyman he remembered being introduced to as "Langley" from Pennsylvania. "I'm hunting for a washroom," he replied with a smile. "I'll see you at the registration table."

Langley smiled in agreement, and Sebastian went on down the stairs, hunting for the cleaning closet, saw a door and pulled it open.

He came up almost slam-bang into what had to be Willie Gurnt, for that long shaft of blond hair shaped almost like a scythe was poking into his right eye just as the photograph had shown. The room was full of buckets, swabs and brushes and smelled strongly of ammonia.

"Jacob?" Gurnt said in a casual, unassuming tone, as if Sebastian were no more than a delivery man.

"Right," Sebastian said amiably, glad for some warm contact here. Gurnt began immediately, then, to help him out of his topcoat and then the suitcoat. "You are Willie Gurnt?" he went on in German.

"Yes. But here I am known as Oscar Brendt, special driver and custodian for the Jubilee Week," he replied. "You don't have much time here. There is a K.G.B. man who would normally have stopped you at the top of the stairs, but he has a regular pattern of visiting the washroom. . . . He wears a blue suit, always blue. . . . He will be watching you while you are here . . ."

"Why is that?" It was obvious why, but he needed Gurnt's experience now.

"The K.G.B. is excited about Udal," Gurnt said and handed Sebastian the starchy white undervest, then the black one to go over it.

"In what way?"

"I got it from Obenoff, Udal's assistant at the church. . . . The K.G.B. have been in and out of the church in the last week asking about Udal. Must be that Udal gave them the slip in Wittenberg."

"Why would the K.G.B. be following him?" Sebastian asked, removing his trousers and taking the black ones Gurnt held out.

"It is a practice of the Soviet Secret Police to cover the movements of anyone who is handling top security assignments for them," Gurnt replied. "The K.G.B. never trusts anyone, even their own. . . . Anyway, Udal has been a question mark in their minds for some time probably . . ."

"All right, but why should Udal, then, give them the slip?" Sebastian insisted on knowing. "The way I get it, he's supposed to have come back into town yesterday, and the Gehlen boys were to snatch him at dawn this morning and put him on ice until next Sunday when he goes out in my place on the bus . . ."

"Maybe he did come in and the Gehlen boys are holding him somewhere else," Gurnt conceded, but not with much confidence. "Anyway, the K.G.B. will be relieved, I think, to see you in your seat tonight, but Colonel

Chekhov is going to want some answers. . . . By the way, your seat number is Row Fourteen, Seat Sixteen . . . that's on the aisle . . ."

"Right," Sebastian said, not liking Udal's possible hanky-panky with the K.G.B. in Wittenberg. It was one of those strings coming loose out of the tight ball of the operation.

"The shoes next," Gurnt said. His voice was dry and unemotional, his words slow and deliberate, as if he were afraid Sebastian might not understand the German. He was not tall—his head came up to the level of Sebastian's nose—but his movements were sure, efficient, like a surgeon handling a scalpel. Gurnt was a pro, no doubt about it, even though his shortness and leanness of figure gave the impression of a straw easily breakable in the wind. His eyes were large but uninterested, a neutral blue-green actually, reflecting a store clerk's boredom with handling too familiar merchandise. It would take a lot to get Willie Gurnt excited—there was some assurance in that, anyway.

"I'll take your papers now," he said as Sebastian fitted in the ruff. Sebastian hesitated a second as he reached into his coat on the chair and took out his passport and East Berlin pass. It was like giving his life away, surrendering all he had left of Raymond Sebastian. But he handed them over finally, and Gurnt took them without a blink of the eye, handing Udal's back in return.

"The last bridge," he said to Gurnt, but there was no hint of compassion for his position.

"There is a phone upstairs in the lobby marked 'Service,'" Gurnt added. "You can phone me here if you find yourself in trouble. Don't use it unless you have to. At ten o'clock tonight break away from the meeting. I will drive you back to the church."

"How do I get hold of you otherwise?"

"You have my number in your papers . . . memorize it and destroy the paper as soon as you can. Again, do not call me unless it is an emergency."

"When can I expect Margot Schell to call?"

Gurnt did not say anything immediately. He was checking over Sebastian's dress very carefully. "She called at the rectory three or four times this week. That's why I'm sure the K.G.B. is worried about Udal. She never calls on Udal during the day—only at night. So I think she will be looking for you soon."

"Well, you can do me a favor and call me each night around eleven o'clock," Sebastian said in a kind of offhand manner, not expecting to be taken seriously. "You might get me out of a jam with the *Fräulein* . . . it's worth a try, anyway, yes?"

Gurnt merely flicked a glance over him, apparently not comprehending why he, Sebastian, would want to be disturbed in any kind of "jam" with a girl like Margot Schell—especially in the light of what was known about Udal's relationship with her.

"It is time now," he said then. "The K.G.B. man is probably back on the stairs . . . he will want to know what you are doing down here. Just tell him that you, Udal, are a member of the East Berlin host committee for the Jubilee and you are checking on facilities."

Gurnt pinned the blue-and-white badge with Kurt Udal's name and the word "Official" on his lapel. "What will that demand of me?" Sebastian asked, feeling the pressure rising.

"Nothing . . . there are thirty others just like you. You are nothing more than an official greeter."

They were finished now. Sebastian would have wanted five more minutes to get to know Gurnt better. But Gurnt was not allowing it. He pointed to the suitcases in the corner. "What for?" Sebastian asked.

"You just got back from Wittenberg, remember?" Gurnt reminded him. "According to a check with Obenoff at five o'clock tonight you hadn't shown up yet." Sebastian got Obenoff straight in his mind from the rogues' gallery of characters he had memorized with Johnny: He was an old man in his seventies that the parish had kept on a pittance to assist Udal in the business end of things.

"How do I say I got back from Wittenberg?" Sebastian insisted, trying to plug up the holes as he saw them coming now.

Gurnt gave him an orange folder that said: "Rent a Skoda—From Wittenberg to Berlin." "This is the way the Gehlen boys said Udal would come back," Gurnt explained. "You will see the route marked on the map. He was supposed to stop at Spindlersfeld to visit a friend named Otto Selznick. Repeat it, please . . ." Sebastian did so. "Now whether Udal did or not is not our problem right now. . . . You will find the license number of the car on the folder too, and the rental agent here in Berlin where Udal was to drop the car off . . ."

"But we are not sure he did, are we?"

"They should have told you on the other side about that," Gurnt said, the first cloud of irritation crossing these bland, watery eyes. For Sebastian it was like seeing his own doctor frowning over a stethoscope held to his chest. It was another frayed edge. "It is too late now to wait for the check. You'll just have to play it as if he did. Now, good luck!"

He was out in the hall again, having the sensation of being shoved out onto a stage in the glare of the footlights, confused about his lines. He stood there a few seconds, hearing the rumble of conversation upstairs, the sound of instruments being tuned for the evening performance. Otto Selznick of Spindlersfeld. Nothing like that had been fed into his mental computer by Johnny. It seemed too important to miss—why wasn't he told about Udal's plans in Wittenberg?"

What did Johnny once say to him? "Better men than you, ten times better, better thinkers, have tried this and failed . . ." Well, if it blew up, it would happen in the next five minutes or five hours at the most.

He walked upstairs. The heavy-set man in the blue suit was there at the top as Gurnt had said he would be. He was reading a newspaper and chewing gum, his flabby jowels quivering like pudding. He put out one big meaty hand and stopped Sebastian, then looked at his badge, his small, dark eyes dilating a little as he realized who he was. "Checking facilities," Sebastian said as Gurnt had instructed him. The man stopped chewing for a long minute, and Sebastian could see where he'd missed shaving on his chin that morning. Those dark eyes moved from the badge to Sebastian's face, and Sebastian hoped that the sweat didn't show up too much on his upper lip—and above all else, he hoped the American named Langley didn't stroll up right now.

The K. G. B. man went back to his chewing slowly, then said, "Go on," and Sebastian continued up the steps to the main foyer and the registration area. He found his official program packet in the basket marked "officials." Glancing back, he saw the K. G. B. man on the phone. The word was going out: Udal had returned. How long now before Margot Schell or even Chekhov moved in on him?

He spent some time in the upper-floor washroom and at 7:28 went to his seat. Nobody approached him. He played it as cool as he could, sweating out the few long minutes till the overture. The stage finally filled with dignitaries, the lights dimmed and the orchestra struck up "A Mighty Fortress Is Our God." He could relax now for the next hour and half.

He got nothing out of the opening ceremonies, thinking of his next moves, backtracking, wondering if Udal got back from Wittenberg, how he would handle Margot Schell. Then it was over. The lights went on again. A tall, lean clergyman, his voice loud as a cannon shot, was giving the benediction. The orchestra played a fitting retreat and he got up, preparing for the handshakes.

Happily, the identification badges had big, grease-pencil lettering. When someone approached him in a friendly way, he would glance at the name and go into effusive greeting as he figured Udal would have done, as he did in those films. When he found himself getting into conversation beyond his knowledge, he found ways to excuse himself for other "pressing duties" as host.

He went at it like that for a full hour, through coffee, now and then making it to the washroom so he wouldn't have the constant pressure of trying to wend his way through conversation loaded with booby traps. And all the time the K.G.B. man was in the background, chewing that gum as if he were trying to beat some record.

By ten o'clock he was bone weary with it all; his eyes smarted, his mouth was parched, his tongue sore from sucking wind through his teeth in that peculiar habit of Udal's when he talked, and his lips and jaw muscles felt limp from keeping that smile of Udal's pasted together. And he knew the law of averages would catch up with him. One of the nine hundred delegates crowded into the cathedral was bound to drop an egg in his lap—some insignificant point of history, of past meetings, a name thrown in he should know, especially if he was asked by a security plant. And his mind was beginning to act like backed-up plumbing. It was too dangerous to try to meet any more challenges in his present state, so when he found himself with a crowd blocking the view of the omnipresent K.G.B. man, he made his move out and down into the lower foyer.

He got Gurnt on the phone, and five minutes later he had the car waiting out front. The K.G.B. man caught up to him by then, but he didn't stop him. After all, Udal with two suitcases deserved a ride home at the least. But once on their way, Gurnt warned him that the K.G.B. seemed to be everywhere.

"I checked the rental garage," Gurnt added. "The car which Udal was supposed to drive according to the brochure did not check in yet. But another car from Wittenberg got in at three this afternoon. Our man inside the place made out a new receipt with your name on it—it will take some time for your friend, Colonel Chekhov, to track it down to the original bill in Wittenberg. Here is the license number of the car . . ."

Gurnt gave him the number, and he wrote it beside the

other after scratching out the original.

"Aren't you underestimating Chekhov?" Sebastian asked.

Gurnt shrugged. "I never underestimate Chekov. All this will do is buy time. It could be he won't start the check back immediately, because the license number and receipt will show up at the rental agency. He will have to be very suspicious to check the original in Wittenberg."

"Where is Udal then?" Sebastian prodded.

"Maybe in another place the Gehlen boys haven't bothered to tell us about . . . which wouldn't be the first time they did that."

Nothing more was said. Sebastian saw the Reformation Church coming up now to his left across from the big department store. Gurnt swung back across the street and into the wide-open gate and up the cracked, potholed drive to the rectory. It was a sizable church with a high spire and bell tower, lit up by the department store neon signs kitty-corner across the street. It had a peaked roof and the usual gray-white cement siding that characterized these old European churches.

He got out and said, *"Auf Wiedersehen!"* to Gurnt. Then, as the car pulled out of the drive, he walked through a breezeway and into a small courtyard to the rear of the church that was supposed to be a kind of garden. A bulb burned feebly on a rusty iron post; it was typical of the decay here.

He tested the doorknob first before hunting for the key that had been made for him on the other side. To his surprise, he found the door open. He pushed in cautiously. There was no light. Before he could find it, the lamp switched on in front of him. He blinked for a minute, catching the room in one swift glance, seeing old leather chairs, a coffee table stacked with magazines, an old upright piano to his right against the wall, a frayed greenish rug that covered the floor, and a fireplace whose low coals sputtered a feeble attempt at cheer. And there was the smell of cigarette smoke too.

Then he saw her. She was sitting behind the lamp that was perched on a small, rickety desk. He wanted to stare at her, but his instincts told him he had to play it casual. She had on a white turtle-neck sweater, and her long wheat-colored straight hair tumbled over it in a careless cascade of girlishness. There was only a trace of a smile on her frosted lips, and the smoke from her cigarette undulated in front of her like a cobra mesmerized by her compelling beauty. His first thought was that she was more beautiful than the film had shown her to be.

"Welcome home, darling!" she said, her voice betraying a determined effort to cover up something he couldn't quite detect. "Dear Obenoff, he was so kind to let me in. Do you mind?" A nerve began to pound in Sebastian's neck as he kicked his suitcases inside. It was happening too soon. He wanted the night to himself, to recoup his mental forces and put a lid on his choppy emotions. He tried to smile, pulling off his topcoat and tossing it across the battered leather chair by the door. He went to the fire immediately to poke it up, because he knew he had to keep busy, to stay away from her.

"It is nice of you," he said to her, digging into the coals with the poker, knowing that it sounded pretty weak.

"Nice?" she said from behind him, her voice modulated now to a tone of amusement. "Anything we have had together, dear Kurt, has been much more than nice—so is it suddenly to be nothing more now?" He didn't answer, unsure of what their relationship had been up to now. He felt her move behind him then. "You were playing it naughty this time?" she went on, her voice still well back toward the desk.

"Why?" he responded, trying to play it coy.

"Put that poker down and look at me, Kurt," she commanded him then, and he slowly hung the poker back on the hook and turned to face her. She was half sitting, half leaning against the desk, her arms folded across her sweater, the cigarette still smoking between the fingers of her left hand. She had on a brown tweed skirt that came down to about an inch above her knees, showing off a pair of good legs, not heavy with muscles as he had seen in many German women who looked as if they had worked the fields too long; there was a delicate shape to hers that came with a lean diet and bicycle riding. If he could relax and view her leisurely, he knew it would be a delightful experience. But as it was, every line of her was a disturbing contribution to her sureness, to her image of proficiency as a worker inside the East German government. "You made a stupid move in Wittenberg, shaking off the K.G.B. . . . I have told you often never to try that. It means I must explain for you—"

"Let them ask about it," he cut back, trying now to get into his Udal role as he figured she would expect of him.

"Why did you do it?" she asked, peering at him intently with her eyes turning to a luminous blue-black.

"I get tired of having to take them along wherever I go," he returned mildly.

She snorted and tossed her hair with a shake of her head, a gesture of exasperation. "All this time you have been an agent of the K.G.B., and suddenly you decide to pull such an amateurish trick like that. Chekhov won't accept that, and you know I cannot. Where did you go?"

"I rented a car on my own and visited a friend in Spindlersfeld. That's all there is to it, Margot. Check it out if you want to . . ."

"We will have to, of course," she replied shortly. She said nothing more, continuing to half sit there on the edge of that spindly desk, watching him, while he tried to think up ways to get off the impaling hook of her probing questions and her intense scrutiny of him. Then, very quietly, she said, "Aren't you even going to kiss me?"

There it was. It was as if he heard Johnny laugh there in the room. How did he play it now? How far was he ready to go for another man's life? For the Pentateuch, if there was any truth to the manuscript's being here at all? What was in a kiss, anyway? Nothing, except maybe that no two men kissed alike. Beyond that was that other thing, what Johnny said he couldn't do in the same situation—refuse to go down as far as he had to to make a few scores for God. But it was his own life now, too, riding on this. As much as he had thought about the confrontation in days past, as much as he had convinced himself that the choice of action would be simple, now that it was here he found himself hesitating, caught in the implications of a move either way.

He turned and took the poker off the wall again, going back to digging in the fire, fighting for time, hoping for some kind of detour in the road. "I've been doing some thinking," he tried, and he knew it wasn't very good. "I guess Wittenberg helped me to bring it to a head. I think maybe we should slow down . . . in what we have together."

He felt her move across the room toward him, and when he caught the scent of her perfume that contained just a hint of the sweet springlike freshness of arbutus, he knew she was directly behind him.

"What happened in Wittenberg?" she said to him, and her voice was so close to his right ear that the warmth of her breath touched it, caressing his neck. Sweat glued his shirt to his back now, and the poker felt greasy in his hand. He put it back onto the hook and moved away from her. "Stand still, Kurt!" she snapped at him, and he stopped a few feet from her, jamming his suddenly cold hands deep into his trouser pockets, keeping half-turned toward her. "Look at me . . ."

He turned slowly around until his eyes met hers, and he saw the steady, relentless probing there. "Now tell me what happened?"

He sighed and looked at the floor, avoiding those eyes that had a way of looking straight into his mind. "I know you won't understand, but I've been feeling lately that maybe I should be paying more attention to my vows—"

Her laugh flowed out of her in ripples of ridicule like water out of a bottle.

"Anything but that, darling Kurt," she said snidely. "Anything but a spiritual experience coming from you who are far beyond recall. . . . I am not a child, you know. All that we have had here cannot be wiped out with so crude a statement." She threw her half-smoked cigarette into the fireplace, then, and approached to within a few feet of him. There was nothing he could do but stand there looking into her eyes, seeing himself deep in them, noting the softness of the skin on her face, the delicate lines of her nose, the wide curve of her full-lipped mouth, the lower lip caught between two beautiful teeth as she looked up at him, pondering, her eyes filled with mock amusement and accusation. She reached up to put her hands on his shoulders, and he put his hands on her arms in a gesture that could be interpreted as affection but was really used to keep her arms from going up around his neck. "You seem different to me, you are more subdued, even look different," she said, her breath warm on his chin. "Your eyes are tired, your face is thinner. . . . I am a poor loser, Kurt. I do not like to give you up to anyone or anything, not even God, who I can't believe I have competition with . . . not in your case. But I can wait for the answers about Wittenberg . . ."

He felt her arms tighten in his grip and move up on his shoulders. And he knew she would kiss him then—there wouldn't be a thing he could do about it. And though the warning signals burned the circuits in his brain, he almost felt as though it had to be.

Then the phone slashed into the room with an abrupt, clanging, ripping sound, like a shot in a tomb. She didn't relax her grip on his neck though, and her eyes were slowly closing in anticipation of the kiss. The phone cut in again.

"Let it ring," she whispered hoarsely.

"Could be my contact," he said with a kind of tight croak in his voice, jarred out of the moment of complete dominance by her, but careful not to move too quickly. Slowly he lifted her arms, stepped away from her and headed for the phone. He picked up the receiver, stood there a minute to steady his breath and said, "Yes?"

"This is Oscar Brendt at the cathedral, Herr Udal," Gurnt's voice had that listless, disinterested tone of his, and Sebastian suppressed a sigh of relief. "There is business here at the church . . . could you come and help set up the program packets and arrange for a few other details yet this evening?"

He turned toward her now. She had her back to the fireplace, to watch him, so he said, "Right now?" putting a frown on his face to lend credence to his dismay.

"I am sorry," Gurnt said shortly.

"All right, I will be there in five minutes." He hung up, and she turned around to stare at the fire. He picked up his topcoat and stood there a moment, wondering what she really was thinking.

"They want me to do some checking about the program right away," he told her. She didn't move, and he thought maybe he should walk up behind her and touch his lips to her neck, to affirm what they once had. But he knew any move of that kind could overpower him—so he started toward the door. Suddenly it was flung open, slamming into the wall with a jarring force, and the cold night air rushed in, rattling loose papers and carrying with it a harbinger of evil. Two Russian military police in their green overcoats stepped in smartly and stood at attention on either side of the door. Sebastian waited a few seconds, wondering, then a slightly built man in an olive-colored officer's uniform walked in. He stood there a minute looking at them, an empty, red cigarette holder gripped firmly between his teeth, jutting upward toward his right eye as if it were stuck in his lower jaw. On his chest were four rows of medals. His black boots shone like metal and his breeches were perfectly fitted. There was in his bearing a manner that characterized Soviet military history of the last twenty years or so—proud, confident, ruthless. But in him it was polished to a fine sheen by top echelon duties which Johnny had once said "could make bar-

barians into counts." He slowly removed a gold-trimmed monocle from his right eye, bowed slightly and clicked his heels together.

"I regret this intrusion," he said, his German rather clumsy, his voice high pitched, and his smile a leer wrapped around that empty cigarette holder. "Herr Udal, I have followed your movements for a long time, but unfortunately we have never met. I am Colonel Gregor Chekhov, military attaché to the K.G.B. Security Division. You will please to put your coat down?"

Sebastian looked at Margot Schell off to his left where she had turned from the fireplace. She showed no sign of agitation at Chekhov's entry; it was as if she had expected it. They stood there, none of them moving except for Chekhov, who began to remove his black gloves a finger at a time in the careful, methodical manner of an executioner. Sebastian cleared his throat noisily and dropped his coat on the chair. The two guards closed the door on a signal from Chekhov and waited at attention. Suddenly the room became very close, very still.

* 6 *
Who's Got the Joker?

Chekhov moved around the room as if he were browsing in an antique shop, slapping his gloves into his right hand now and then.

"You will please to tell me, Herr Udall, why you deliberately fled your K.G.B. escort a week ago yesterday, Saturday, to be exact, in Wittenberg?" he asked, and he paused to study a photograph of Udal in front of his church.

"I wanted to visit my friend in Spindlersfeld without having to explain to my bodyguard," Sebastian responded politely.

"What friend is that?"

"Otto Selznick . . ."

"What does he do?"

"Do?"

"Yes—what trade, occupation?"

Sebastian didn't know, but he took a chance with, "He's a laborer," remembering that Spindlersfeld was in Kopenick and Johnny had told him in his geography lesson that Kopenick was an industrial area.

"Laboring at what?" Chekhov picked up a piece of blue china from the desk and examined it carefully.

"I do not know . . . I didn't ask."

"How did you get here from Wittenberg?"

Sebastian reached inside his coat and took out the orange brochure on the Skoda rental service. "I rented a car, a Skoda," he said, and held out the brochure toward Chekhov, who looked up and then walked over slowly to take it. He was but a few feet from Sebastian now, his greenish eyes fastened on his face. The right one that needed the monocle was almost glazed over with a peculiar watery film. There were small lines in the narrow face, under the eyes and at the corners of the thin mouth. His nose twitched like a rabbit's, as if he were getting ready for a good sneeze, and his mouth kept puckering moodily.

He examined the brochure a full minute in silence. "The license number of the car?"

"It it written there . . ."

"You scratched one number out and put another on top . . . why?"

"A mistake," Sebastian said simply, and he cleared his throat again as a spongy pocket of phlegm formed there.

"This route you have marked as having traveled," Chekhov went on, "it is a secondary road . . . why did you take that instead of the main line into Kopenick?"

"To avoid the police who I was sure would be looking for me," Sebastian returned blandly enough.

"Is this friend so important that you would risk trouble with the K.G.B. just to see him in private?"

"Otto Selznick is a respected friend of the family. . . . I didn't want him to know I was working for the K.G.B."

Chekhov sniffed, then turned and handed the Skoda brochure to one of the guards. He took to walking around the room again. "You know the penalty for evading the K.G.B. escort, Herr Udal?" he asked. Sebastian didn't answer, because he didn't know. Chekhov stopped by the small desk and looked back at him. "It can mean a very long imprisonment . . . such action is taken to be on the same level as counterespionage. Is that not right, Fräulein Schell?"

Sebastian saw her move forward from the fireplace and pause a few feet behind and to the right. "It means he could be shot," she said simply, and Sebastian looked at her quickly, for she said that as though she were trying to get Chekhov to agree. Chekhov smiled around the cigarette holder.

"Are you suggesting I do that, *Fräulein?*" he asked.

Margot straightened her shoulders and looked at Sebastian. "I have warned him, Colonel. . . . I am reminding him again of the seriousness of pranks like that."

"Yes," Chekhov agreed, "and for this reason I find your desire for freedom, Herr Udal, a very stupid one and hardly believable considering your record with the K.G.B. . . . This will demand careful study, yes, very careful study." He paused now and advanced toward Sebastian again, stopping those same few feet away, looking down at his boots, checking the shine, his hands now behind his back. "You are a man of the Bible, Herr Udal," he added then. "What do you know about Jacob and Esau?"

Sebastian dug his toes hard into his shoes, controlling any flinch, any ripple of his muscles.

"In what way, Colonel?"

Chekhov's eyes came up to study his face again, frowning. "I have been monitoring a radio broadcast every evening for the last six weeks," he said abruptly. 'It is always the Genesis account of Jacob and Esau. It intrigues me, this . . . for five minutes only comes the broadcast, never long enough to get a fix on the receiver. What do you make of it?"

"Perhaps a religious zealot trying to get a message of God to East Berliners," Sebastian offered.

"Ah!" Chekhov responded with a lift of his eyebrows, and he removed his cigarette holder now. "But why Jacob and Esau night after night? Christianity is not centered on such a text, is that not right?"

Sebastian sensed that Chekhov could be probing him about his theological beliefs, seeking to match the answers with what he knew about Udal's Biblical knowlege. He fought to remember the drill he had had on Udal's theology with Johnny back at the castle. Finally he shrugged, licking at a dribble of sweat from his upper lip. "Sometimes the Jacob and Esau story can be of great comfort in certain conditions . . ."

Chekhov simply continued to study him, saying nothing. The room was very still now, heavy with the kind of tension that builds when a man is dismantling the timing device on a bomb. Sebastian felt the pincers closing on him in the room, for Chekhov was getting too close—did he already know and was he playing cat and mouse?

Chekhov slowly put his cigarette holder back into his mouth, then turned and bowed quickly to Margot Schell and proceeded to the door, which a guard swung open for him. He paused there, with the night air swirling in around him like a friendless ghost looking for a séance, and pulled on his black gloves with the same care as when he took them off. "We will check the car, the route you took from Wittenberg, Herr Udal," he said crisply. "You have the Jubilee Week ahead of you, but when it is over you will have to endure the pleasantries of our office to give a full account. . . . Until then, may I urge you to walk carefully? We do not intend to allow another escapade like this to happen again. Meanwhile, your East German travel permit is revoked. I regret such stringency, but we do not allow our K.G.B. men to wander at will. Now, then, *auf Wiedersehen!*"

Sebastian stood there a long time after the door had closed and the sound of the military boots faded into the night. Margot had found a cigarette on the desk top and had lit it with a paper match. Sebastian picked up his coat and headed for the door.

"Shall I wait?" she asked him quietly.

He paused at the door, his hand on the knob, staring down at his knuckles turning white where they gripped. He glanced quickly back at her and put on the grin Udal used for a now-you-laugh-here aura. "I would like nothing better," he said lightly. "But I think this is going to be a long session . . ."

"Dinner Tuesday night at the Imperial as usual?" she countered, and the tone was jabbing now. She wasn't liking this, his diffidence, his noncommitment, his trying to break what relationship they had been experiencing up to now. He would like to think it was her wounded pride, but he wasn't sure it wasn't more testiness in not being able to square him up in her mind.

"The Jubilee will keep me running, Margot," he said, and then quickly added, "but I'm sure I can find a way to meet you at the Imperial."

"Don't patronize me, Kurt," she returned with a smile that was about as warm as a Russian tank driver's.

He nodded, gave her a quick smile again and said, "Then, about eight at the Imperial?" and went out, not waiting for the answer.

He walked rapidly the three blocks to the cathedral, his shoulders back, his head up like Udal's, glad for the touch of frost in the air that helped cool his boiling blood. His legs were a solid ache now, his head throbbed, and a stupefying weariness assaulted him. He should be asleep building up the energy he'd need for tomorrow, not clippety-clopping down this dark street with its shadows and lurking evil. But he wanted to see Gurnt anyway; he had to make contact. Everything was going too fast. At this rate, he wouldn't last till Wednesday.

But Willie Gurnt had no sympathy. At least he didn't show any. He leaned, arms folded, against the wall of that ammonia-smelling cubicle in the cathedral basement while he listened to Sebastian. His heavy lids drooped, like those of a frog getting ready to doze.

"The question is," Sebastian concluded, "does Chekhov know? Why would he pull that Jacob and Esau bit out of the air? If he knows, why doesn't he arrest me now and get it over with?"

"He does not know," Gurnt said quietly, categorically. "If he knew, he would have the K.G.B. running to every corner of Germany to find the real Udal. He still accepts you, what you said . . ."

Sebastian swallowed that grudgingly, then added, "What about the Imperial Tuesday night? Can I use the Jubilee to pass up Margot Schell?"

Gurnt thought a moment, looking at the floor, as though getting ready to spit. "You are not like Udal," he said.

"How do you mean?"

"You are too sensitive with the *Fräuleins*, yes?" and Gurnt's eyes came up now to fasten on him as if Sebastian were a piece of faulty merchandise he had been stuck with.

Sebastian smiled. "I am sensitive to *this Fräulein*, Herr Gurnt," he replied.

"You are a pastor like Udal, yes?"

"Not exactly like Udal. I don't particularly care to romp in bed even with so charming a woman as Margot Schell—"

"Then you should not have come," Gurnt said tersely. "This is no place for a puritan—"

"I know, I know," Sebastian shot back, lifting his hand to ward off any more of that. "I was told that at great length on the other side."

"Then you will have to play along with the *Fräulein*, even like Udal," Gurnt said flatly. "It is too dangerous not to do it, yes? I cannot use the telephone any more like tonight—she is a very clever woman who can tell when the wind blows off the swamps."

Sebastian nodded, for he, too, knew that there was no other way, that he would have to trust his own escape routes when it came to her. "This man Udal," he added, "must be quite an operator . . . fast with the *Fräuleins* and all that."

Gurnt looked at him blankly as if not comprehending. "You call it corruption perhaps," he said. "But we call it expediency. We learn to survive—that is our main concern. We are not fortunate here to have a choice of what you call moral values. Udal works both sides of the wall, so he has even fewer choices." He sniffed as if bothered by the ammonia and said, "We can go up now."

"One thing more, and I'll drop it," Sebastian restrained him. "Won't the K.G.B. get suspicious when Sebastian's auditorium seat and hotel room aren't filled? And there's an American named Langley who came over on the bus with me who seems to be too friendly and too concerned about my welfare. Isn't he going to start wondering?"

A frown cut across Gurnt's languid eyes, signifying he didn't like to be cross-examined. "Your papers were copied before we sent them on to the Gehlen contact for Udal," he said coolly, his hand on the doorknob. "They are good enough to pass a Volkspolizei check. We have a man in your place in the hotel assigned you—he is there only to pass the head count. If they check his identification, we might have trouble—but chances are the K.G.B. won't. As to Langley, there are too many delegates for him to be concerned about one—anyway, he is probably in another hotel. The K.G.B. doesn't like all Americans in one place. Anyway, I will do the thinking for us on these matters, Herr Udal."

Sebastian bowed his acknowledgment of Gurnt's efficiency, then followed him out the door and up to the auditorium. By now—past midnight—all the visiting clergymen had taken to their hotels. Only a few custodians worked in the outer foyer. The place was empty.

Sebastian followed Gurnt to the platform, and they went through the motions of arranging the next day's program packets. It was after one when Gurnt finished his work and sat down at the grand piano to the left of the stage. Sebastian watched him as he began playing "Clair de Lune," the notes coming off softly and expertly. Then he rumbled into the *Tannhäuser* overture. As he concentrated on the music, his face seemed to soften, and the fatigue that added years to the mouth and chin seemed to go away. He took on a boyish look, the hook point of his yellow hair jumping with his movements, dipping into his eyes. Sebastian moved slowly to the piano and stood leaning against it, watching him, fascinated by the alteration. Gurnt was driving his long, tapered fingers into the music as if writing the score himself, his eyes half-closed. The overture ended, and Gurnt ran his fingers over the keys in a carefree sounding of chords.

"Where'd you learn that?" Sebastian asked, then, feeling it was safe now to intrude. Gurnt paused, suddenly becoming conscious of where he was. He stared at his fingers poised over the keys in seeming disbelief.

"Who knows?" he said aloofly. "It comes from somewhere in the past, some great-grandfather perhaps . . ."

"Piano lessons at thirteen?" Sebastian asked lightly, wanting to know more of this strange man with his double-edged personality.

Gurnt thumped the chords in one loud finale and got up quickly to gather in a few packets and start for the auditorium exit. He paused a moment, looking back at Sebastian, weighing the question as if it hadn't been put to him before. "At thirteen I was in a Hitler suicide defense unit, aiming a bazooka at a Red tank in Potsdamer Platz . . ." His eyes wandered to the floor in front of him as if he were seeing it all there again. Then, glancing wryly at Sebastian, his eyes still showing traces of the excitement the music had produced in him, he said, "No, there wasn't much time for piano lessons. Such things have been and always will be a luxury. I learned to play from the inside. I play to find my soul, perhaps like other East Berliners who look for it in a woman, an extra pack of black-market cigarettes or like the Grepos who shoot people trying to jump the wall. You learn to get good at what you think will give you meaning in life . . . like you with God, yes?"

He turned then and walked up the aisle to the rear of the auditorium. After a minute Sebastian followed, the piano notes still reverberating from the high sculptured ceiling.

Gurnt drove him home at 1:30. Margot Schell had gone. He got pajamas out of one of the suitcases and went into the bedroom. The bed· was neatly turned down; Obenoff again. He climbed into bed, pulling up the covers against the chill in the room. He flicked off the bed lamp and let the shadows come down on him. A pale glow from the light in the garden outlined the narrow window and gave the room a murky dimness, exaggerating the strange bulkiness of the simple furniture. He tried to sleep, but his mind kept slipping from Sebastian to Udal. As he lay there, he found it even more difficult to detach himself from Udal: the room, the strong smell of soap in the sheets, the musty odor of the mattress, the odor of Udal himself, the tobacco smoke hanging stale in the room, the heavy pine scent of cologne . . . and he felt that peculiar ripple of excitement as the shape of Margot Schell came floating toward him like a jinni out of a bottle with that teasing scent of arbutus. And he thought of what Udal must have had going with her; how simple it would be to play his role to the fullest with such a beautiful woman. . . .

But then his eyes snapped open. He sat up quickly on the edge of his bed, his heart hammering, his bare feet touching the cold tiles of the floor. He was giving way to Udal too quickly. His will to remain Sebastian was being diluted in his battle to stay alive here. He was in the same struggle as Johnny—only Johnny had never had to come this far. And he was afraid Margot Schell was going to succeed in her attempt to finally strip him of his armor.

He lay back in bed a long time, pondering the issue, driving his thoughts back to Sebastian, reminding himself again and again who he was, until he felt himself slip into the soft cotton of sleep.

He woke with a start, letting his eyes take in the room, trying to establish surroundings. The sun was hitting the window now, and the room was sharpened with new light. The clock read 7:15. He saw the tray on the side table with the coffeepot and cup and two hard rolls with a bottle of jam. That would be Obenoff already on the job.

He got up quickly, wanting to get shaved and dressed and fully alert before he had to meet the old man. Besides that, he wanted to get to the cathedral, feeling it would be safer than here, where the proximity to Udal's life could bring more serious slips.

He had dressed and was finishing his coffee in the parlor when Obenoff walked in, a stoop-shouldered figure with thin, gray-white hair and a shrunken face. A pair of old, twisted glasses balanced on the tip of his large nose, and a poorly fitted black suit hung on the skeletal frame as if his body were no more than a clothes hanger.

"I am glad to see you back, Pastor," he said indifferently, and it was obvious that there had never been any rapport between him and Udal.

Sebastian grunted a reply and finished his coffee. He hung onto his cup as a prop, wanting to be on his way before too many questions were asked—-but it was only a little after eight, and the Jubilee didn't start until nine.

"Some of the people asked for counsel with you on Thursday," Obenoff continued as he moved painfully around the room, attempting to straighten what really didn't need straightening.

"You handle them," Sebastian said abruptly. "The Jubilee will take all my time this week."

Obenoff paused in his work and turned his head slowly, peering over his glasses with those washed-out eyes which said clearly enough that Udal seldom, if ever, relegated such duties to his assistant. Sebastian knew he had overstepped himself.

"What about the Catechism for the boys at four?" Obenoff asked.

"I will hardly have time this week," Sebastian returned coolly.

Obenoff went on idly dusting the books on the shelf. "What will I do with them, then?" he queried, his voice cracking with concern. "The Dettmann boy is getting more difficult every day. He seldom shows up for vespers. All of them grow more and more rebellious. These last ten days during your absence were the worst."

Sebastian didn't know about the boys. It was one more imponderable, one more unknown factor that could trip him up.

"Do your best until the Jubilee is finished," he said shortly. Without waiting for an answer, he picked up his coat and headed for the door. He wanted to get out of the room before other questions were asked. Obenoff didn't hold him back.

He went through the garden courtyard and into the church, heading for the Alexanderplatz side. As he entered the nave, he noticed the candles, illuminating the huge altar. He hesitated a moment, not sure what Udal would have done, not sure he should be rushing out during preparation for a service of some sort. He put his coat down on the front pew, walked up to the altar and knelt at the railing, staying there a full minute, hearing only the sputter of the candles and the creaks in the wall that made the whole building sound like a great ship at sea.

When he finally opened his eyes, he noticed the boyish figure not more than ten feet away, half-hidden in the shadows. He held a candelabrum in his right hand, a hymnbook in his left with a carelessness linked to distaste. Sebastian had no idea how long the fellow had been standing in the wings watching him. He couldn't be more than twelve or thirteen years old. Eyes, big and round, studied him out of a waxen face set in lines of pugnaciousness. A dirty white altar robe was wrapped around him carelessly like a smock, the faded red cross in the center set off against the gray in his eyes. There was nothing innocent about that face. The boy had obviously not expected to see Sebastian there and had stopped short on his way to the altar. No doubt it was one of the boys Obenoff had referred to . . . but which one? He would have to ask Gurnt.

Sebastian closed his eyes again, not wanting to confront that character now. When he opened them a few minutes later, the boy was gone. With some relief he got up and headed out down the long central aisle of the church. He caught only a glimpse of a man sitting in the back pew as he made for the door of the street, a single lonely figure with a wind-blown tuft of gray hair and an age-lined face. One brave soul, Sebastian thought, as he went out the door, willing to try for some heat in the only place that offered anything close to promise.

He walked the three blocks to the cathedral in the brisk morning air, feeling some sense of anonymity in the increasing pedestrian and auto traffic at this hour. He put the Udal snap into the military stride, while keeping the black fedora perched squarely on his head, the portfolio clutched under his arm.

When he got there, the K.G.B. man in the blue suit was standing by the stairs, still chewing gum, the newspaper rolled up under his arm. His black eyes studied Sebastian in same pondering way, and Sebastian almost felt there was a humorous twinkle in those eyes, as if the man actually knew who he was and was enjoying Sebastian's attempt at beguilement.

Sebastian would have liked to check in with Gurnt, but he knew the K.G.B. man would follow him down anyway. So he went on up the stairs and had to do a quick move to the right as he saw Langley standing there talking to other American clergymen. Sooner or later, he knew he'd have to prepare for that inevitable confrontation.

He managed to carry out the masquerade that morning well enough, but he was certain now that he was leaving some people with a little puzzlement about him. Now and then he could see groups of men talking and looking his way. He was forced more and more to break out of conversations that seemed to demand of him some kind of knowledge he did not possess. This, he knew, was bound to force the issue very soon, and someone was going to get the word to the K.G.B.

Finally, at four that afternoon, his muscles aching from the tension, he went to the washroom—his fifth trip of the day—and got into a stall and locked the door, for he desperately needed the moment of reprieve. He took his time, letting his hammering pulse quiet down; then he removed his ruff and touched the sores under his hairline and ears. He simply could not get used to it.

After twenty minutes he finally went out, moving across the tile floor. He got up to the basin with its long mirror, and that's when Langley came in. Right behind him was the gum-chewing K.G.B. man. Sebastian shoved his head down into the basin and turned on the cold-water tap. He stayed down, looking back to see where Langley was. The K.G.B. man was standing at the far end of the long line of basins. Sebastian lifted his dripping face, couldn't see Langley and decided to make for the paper towels.

At that moment, Langley came around the corner and strode up to the basin next to him. "Well," he began, smiling into the mirror, "I was just asking where you've been! Haven't seen you since the first night we got in."

Sebastian smiled back, trying to play it dumb. The K.G.B. man was not looking at them, but he was very carefully washing his hands as if he'd gotten a splash of acid on them. "Let's see now—your name is—"

"Excuse me," Sebastian said in German, smiling at Langley, backing away from him, keeping his name tag away from Langley's scrutiny. "I must be going . . ."

"Yes, well, that's all right," Langley smiled, but there was a puzzlement in his eyes now. And the K.G.B. man hadn't missed it either. Sebastian grabbed the paper towels on his way, made a stab at drying his hands, and tossed them into the wastebasket, all in almost the same motion. He was out the door before Langley could call to him.

When he got to the auditorium, he was breathing hard, and the crowding sense of concern was beginning to press on his breastbone. If that K.G.B. man was as smart as he was paid to be, there was going to be some checking with Langley.

The rest of the day, on up to nine that evening, he was able to get through without further incident. But he knew Langley would be waiting to tackle him again, and the K.G.B. were undoubtedly alerted too. At nine, feeling like a trapped animal in a corral, he called Gurnt and asked for a ride home. Gurnt didn't argue with him, figuring Sebastian had something important to talk about.

But in the car Gurnt warned him, "I should not be driving you. They will begin to wonder. Anyway, why do you want to go home so early? Fräulein Schell could be waiting . . ."

"Yes, well, I'll take her over what's building up back in the cathedral," Sebastian said glumly. He told Gurnt about Langley.

Gurnt was silent for a minute and then said, "We will have to perhaps put Langley out of commission for a few days . . ."

"Meaning what?"

"Nothing serious . . . we have our ways."

"Don't hurt him, that's all I ask."

Gurnt's eyes flicked at him in the rear-view mirror, and there was an ingredient of wry amusement there, as if such a request were quite irrelevant to the operation at hand.

"Tell me if you can about the kids Udal has with him in the church," Sebastian went on then. He related what had happened during his prayer time at the altar that morning.

"That would be Christian Dettmann probably," Gurnt said. "He's a kind of leader of the four other boys who are orphans put under Udal's church instruction class. Actually, it is really dialectical materialism Udal teaches them, because Udal has to keep up the front with Communism here. Every year Ulbricht assigns orphans to various institutions for what he calls indoctrination—some of them might get some Christianity, but mostly it is all according to Marx. Dettmann doesn't like Udal, nor do the others. Udal has put the lash to them more than once, since he is no lover of children anyway, and the accidents of German history like Dettmann are monstrosities that try our patience. . . . Anyway, Udal has a mean streak, a little unbecoming to a churchman, yes?"

Sebastian didn't answer, preoccupied instead with the sobering fact of his own identity with Udal.

"One other thing about Dettmann," Gurnt said as Sebastian opened the door to get out. "He's crazy about machines . . . spends most of his time when Udal isn't around watching the construction cranes down on Liebknechtstrasse and Marx-Engels-Platz. If you ever have cause to wonder where he is, try there. . . . Sleep well!"

Inside the rectory, he took a shower that was no more than a few disorganized leaks out of a rusty fixture over the bathtub. He put on a cold, faded blue cotton robe and went to the small cubicle kitchen to heat up water for a cup of Nescafé.

Later, he sat down at the rickety desk to browse through some of the things Udal left behind. The middle drawer of the desk was open, but it revealed nothing but a few pencils and a discarded assortment of pins, paper clips and erasers. The side drawers were locked. He had no idea where the keys would be, so he got a kitchen knife and worked a good ten minutes on the hasp on the upper drawer. When he opened it, there was only one significant object lying naked on the old mahogany bottom—a German luger, black and menacing here among a minister's personal effects. There were two or three shells in the drawer too, but the chamber was empty. He put the gun back and figured it made sense that Udal should have a weapon, working as he did as a double agent.

He worked on the next drawer down, the bottom one, and when he got it open he found himself staring at something that produced a faint ripple along his tired mental circuits. Three cuff links. As he picked them up, he noticed that only two of them matched. What held him now, though, and what made him pick them up and lay them in his palm was their design—all of them red stone shaped into musical notes. There were two shaped into whole notes; the other was a quarter note. He searched in vain through the drawer for the matching quarter note.

He sat there a long time, it seemed, holding those three nondescript pieces of jewelry in his palm as though he expected them to start crawling like ladybugs, while his mind tried to dredge up his memory.

Yes. Richter. Bishop Hans Richter. His cuff link had been of the same color and design. It was a quarter note. Odd. He continued to sit there, unable to drop the apparently insignificant find back into the drawer. What was a man on the western side of the wall doing with a cuff link that matched another man's here on the eastern side? Coincidence? Maybe.

He rummaged in the drawer and pulled out a folded sheet that felt like a map. When he opened it, however, he saw that it was the calendar for November on the bottom with a complete almanac on the top. He noticed a big red grease-pencil circle around the quarter-moon prediction for November 7.

Quarter-moon . . . quarter note. Was there something Richter and Udal had going here that was all tied up in this cuff link and November 7? But what? Udal was going out on the fifth, not the seventh.

He grunted to himself, trying to banish further speculation. So two men liked red cuff links shaped into musical notes. Maybe it was some kind of fraternity. He looked into the drawer for anything else that might be of interest—but all he found was a booklet titled "Contemporary Church Drama."

He put all of it back into the drawer with a disgruntled sniff. He was not about to let his imagination run wild. He was uptight already on just negotiating the Jubilee successfully, and he didn't need or want any more to think about. But after he got into bed, he felt as if a long hand had poked into the room, jabbing him to pay attention. Why did Richter have only *one* quarter-note cuff link, and why did Udal have the same? Only *one*. People just didn't go out and buy cuff links as unique as that and split them up for no reason.

He rolled over in bed and reminded himself to tell it to Gurnt in the morning. Gurnt would know—wise, deliberate, piano-playing Gurnt. The iceman. "Then will I slay my brother Jacob." And that final note of Johnny's, painfully scribbled before he died, suddenly exploded in his brain so that he sat straight up in bed, staring at the dim glow of the window. It was as if a paper bag full of questions had opened and spilled out across the table like so many pieces of a Scrabble game. Was he really caught up in something bigger than Udal? Is that what those cuff links and the weather calendar added up to? Was he in deeper than he realized? Was Johnny after all trying in his dying message to tell him to stay out of it? Did he know about all this—this thing that began to plague him now with a strange sense of foreboding?

He slowly dropped back onto the bed again, forcing himself to sidetrack it in his mind. But he knew it was there. He smelled it. The death that took Johnny., the strange wind he felt at the Hilton that night, now it blew into this room . . . and it became cold and full of shadows here, and he was a child again, afraid, wishing he could put the light back on—for this was no place to die either, in another man's room that smelled of pine cologne and stale tobacco, far from the sound of familiar places. Had he made a mistake? Did he jump into this too soon? Was he to be fooled into a premature grave?

"God, let it all be my imagination, nothing more," he whispered in the dark.

* 7 *
No Neutral Corner

He knew he was not ready to meet Margot Schell at the Imperial Restaurant on Tuesday evening. The atmosphere at the Jubilee had changed considerably during the day. It was as if his discovery of the previous night had opened the gate to a new kind of pressure, the kind that might be expected at chess tournaments—intense maneuvering designed to checkmate the opponent. Delegates went on with their business as usual, listening to long speeches and participating in discussion groups, oblivious.

He thought it might just be his imagination and the result of the poor sleep he'd had the night before, this preoccupation with the cuff link thing and the increasing sense of sinking into a quagmire. But during the morning, at various break times, people began seeking him out—people who asked all kinds of questions that he found more and more difficult to pass off. He was sure they were K.G.B. men out to trap him in some kind of verbal ambush. He saw Langley, too, now and then, roving among the delgates, and he was certain the K.G.B. must have talked to him about the washroom incident.

He had finally gone to Gurnt in the cleaning closet at 11:30, because he had run out of places to hide. He knew Gurnt disapproved of these meetings, since the K.G.B.

wouldn't be fooled forever if they found him down here too often. Sebastian sat down on an empty packing crate and took the moment to revel in the luxury of being out of the pressure, short-lived as it might be. Gurnt sat on his paint cans in a leisurely, unassuming pose, looking as disinterested as a barber at a wig sale, working that long-bladed knife of his over his fingernails.

"We shall have to put your friend Langley out of it," Gurnt said then, as if he had known all along what Sebastian had been up against all morning.

"What does that mean exactly?" Sebastian responded, running a finger under his sweaty, stiff white collar.

Gurnt paused for a long minute, then said, "Kaput."

"I told you I didn't want it that way," Sebastian warned.

Gurnt snapped the long blade back into its holder, stood up and put in into the pocket of his charcoal-colored denims, folding his arms in a gesture of insistence. "It is not what you want; it is what we must do now to prevent Chekhov from bringing Langley face to face with you. . . . It is only a question of time."

"You said there was another way . . ."

Gurnt nodded. "Yes. But I did not count on the K.G.B. escorting Langley to and from his hotel and keeping guard on him all night. . . . Chekhov must have talked to him and isn't taking chances about our getting to him . . . so we will have to try for Langley here in the cathedral . . ."

"It's my head, not yours," Sebastian argued. "Langley does not deserve death for so simple a reaction of his . . . I'll go to Chekhov myself before I let you do it. I'll blow it all sky high before I let you commit murder in my name or in the name of Jacob and Esau. Do I make myself clear, Herr Gurnt?"

For a moment, Gurnt simply studied him as if he hadn't seen him before, as if Sebastian were a strange specimen of animal that had entered his world, while his washed-out bluish eyes seemed to harden in their understanding of what was said. "It is my head too perhaps," he replied quietly, but there was intensity in that voice now. "And maybe others. . . . If Chekhov gets to you, he will sweat it all out of you . . . ."

"Then it might be well to kill me now and protect yourself," Sebastian returned bluntly, knowing now he would have to hold his own with Gurnt if he was to head off the headlong plunge into disaster.

Gurnt bowed his head and looked at his shoes. "It is a code among us in this kind of work to choose the method that will save the operation," he went on doggedly, like an instructor with a stubborn pupil, his voice holding calm and steady, but not relenting in its insistence. "Already it appears the fire is in the kerosene—"

"I don't operate by those rules," Sebastian cut in.

"Whatever you operate by, Pastor, is no concern to me at the moment," Gurnt snapped, and his eyes were shining now as they began to dilate under pressure of his own inner irritation. "You should have been told that in matters like this it remains for your cover to decide the action—"

"Well, they didn't tell me—"

"Then I tell it to you again!" Gurnt retaliated, and his words were hard now, flung out of the springboard of his impatience. "We do not play church here, not in this business! It is check, countercheck—Chekhov makes a move, we make one better. Why has Shattner let you come when you are obviously not prepared to function in this kind of world? You could ruin us all with such foolish religious antiseptics—"

"It's really New Testament," Sebastian countered and smiled at Gurnt, trying to disarm him. "I play it according to my own rule book. You know anything about that?"

"It is not my business to know anything except how to deliver the goods to the Gehlen Bureau—"

"So what do you get out of it?" Sebastian added, noticing the two spots of color under Gurnt's eyes now, like temperature gauges recording his combustion level. "After you murder Langley, does that help you play the piano better?"

"That has nothing to do with it."

"Maybe," and Sebastian stood now, because he knew he ought to be going. "I'm here to deliver the goods too, Willie—don't forget that. But I want to have a clean conscience when I finish. I don't want to climb over bodies just to get Udal out of the city. You have your price; I have mine. You will have to find a cleaner way to do it, that's all there is to it."

Gurnt took it without immediate rejoinder, continuing to study Sebastian while rubbing his right fist against his chin. Then, dropping his hand, he began to make circles on the floor with the toe of his right shoe. "You will have to face up to some hard dealings in the matter," he said quietly and with finality. "We won't let the operation die for your sense of ideals, Pastor. . . . If necessary, we will get both Langley and you. Is that understood?"

He was not the boyish-looking figure now with a sensitive musician's heart. Gurnt was, after all, what his environment and occupation had made him—a killer. The silence was heavy and alienating, and Sebastian wanted to bridge the gap that suddenly yawned between them. He could not afford a rift with his cover man at this stage. But before he could say anything more, the closet door opened and the K.G.B. man stood there peering at them.

"And don't forget to clean the lavatories and set up the sound equipment," Sebastian said to Gurnt, making it sound as if he had been here simply on an "official" check of facilities again. Then he walked on out, not giving the K.G.B. man more than a quick glance.

At four that afternoon, too much disturbed by his run-in with Gurnt and by the increasing pressure he felt at the cathedral, he walked back to the church rectory, wanting to shower and get freshened up for the evening with Margot Schell. He had to disregard his weariness now, his sense of impending disaster. His one aim was to find ways to keep himself ahead of the K.G.B. one day at a time, and he knew he would have to stay out of the Jubilee traffic as much as he could. He had no idea when Chekhov would confront him with Langley. It was strange that Chekhov would wait so long.

As he walked up the walk to the rectory, he heard the piercing shouts from the back courtyard and looked to see the boys kicking the soccer ball across the cobblestones. For a moment he had the urge to join them, to touch something of humanity once, to communicate something of his life to someone else. But he knew he couldn't. He had no idea of how Udal would have done it—but he rather imagined that there wasn't much love between him and those kids. He watched them for a moment—noticing their spindly legs turned red with the nippy air, their battered, oversized shorts hanging on them. All five were hunched over in a pose of apology as though they were sorry they had been born. Even their faces seemed pale and pinched with cold or fear or whatever it was here in East Berlin. Only one of them seemed to stand straight and almost defiant, commanding the others in sharp tones, lashing at them when they failed to kick the ball right—that had to be Dettmann, he was sure, the same boy he had seen behind the altar. There was a vehemence about the boy's every action, even in the way he kicked the ball, as if the whole world could be booted around just like that. There were savagery and frailty in the swing of his wiry body, a furious attack on all the elements that had perhaps made him feel cheated in the life he had.

As he stood there, one of the boys suddenly spotted him and called the warning to the others. They stopped where they were, their heads bowed, as if they expected punishment. Only Dettmann kept bouncing the ball defiantly, refusing to look up or even acknowledge that Sebastian was there watching.

Sebastian went on into the rectory finally, disturbed by what Udal must have done to them to make them behave toward him like that. And he felt frustration, too, in not being free to attempt some positive healing, to fulfill what he as a man of God ought to be doing here.

He headed for the bedroom to change, but as he came to the door, he noticed it was ajar just a few inches. A thin line of sand showed about a foot back from the door into the main room. As it scraped under his shoes, he paused, sensing that something was out of order here. Finally he gave the door a kick and jumped back as the bucket hit the floor in front of him, spilling sand over the linoleum and bouncing finally to one side in a tinny clatter. At the same time, he heard someone come into the room behind him, and he turned to see Obenoff there, his mouth hanging open, frozen in the shock of the moment.

Sebastian bent over and picked up the bucket, realizing that if he had caught the blow as was obviously intended, it would have left him near dead from the concussion.

"Pastor—" Obenoff finally managed to say, his voice shaky and full of awe, and now he came forward jerkily to dutifully check to see if there had been any harm done. "It is unbelievable. I can't imagine—"

"Who did it?" Sebastian asked, sensing that even Obenoff was not totally happy that the trap had been sprung and Udal had apparently escaped.

"It would have to one of the boys, I suppose," Obenoff said with a certain reluctance, trying his best to offer some protection for them.

"Dettmann, you mean?" Sebastian said.

Obenoff got the fireplace shovel and began scooping up the loose sand into the bucket. "I suppose so," he admitted almost mournfully. "He is a boy almost possessed by the devil! But—but it seems it is so hard for him to adjust to things here—to the church—"

"And me?" Sebastian prodded.

Obenoff didn't answer. He finished scooping up what sand he could into the bucket, and then he said, "Shall I bring him to you?"

"No. Forget it."

"Forget it?" Obenoff repeated, not sure he had heard right. "But you always—" And his voice trailed off as he intended to say that Udal had always punished Dettmann before.

Sebastian looked up at the old man quickly, noticing the perplexed frown, the hint of confusion in those soft, watery eyes. "I have to keep an appointment for dinner," Sebastian said to cover for himself. "I'll deal with the boy some other time. Meanwhile, see that this place is locked and nobody gets in here . . . you understand?"

"Of course, Pastor," the old man murmured and did a quiet and quick retreat. Sebastian leaned against the door jamb leading into the bedroom, staring down at the bucket half-full of sand. "Dear God," he said, his voice sounding hollow in the room, "what has Udal done in this place?" And he slammed his fist hard into the plastered wall, glad for the pain of it, glad to feel something here of the agony of the whole business—to stand among so much human carnage but be forced to play the role of the twisted, fallen angel that was Kurt Udal.

In a hopelessly shredded condition of mind and spirit, he took a cab to the Imperial Restaurant at eight o'clock, trying to retrieve his composure for the company of Margot Schell. As he rode, he noticed the streets jammed with army vehicles, some parked, some moving. He took a chance and asked the driver about it. The eyes in the rear-view mirror flicked a look at him as if to say he should know better. Then the driver explained that the Russians had brought in crack divisions for a special parade to celebrate the anniversary of the Russian Revolution.

When he arrived at the hotel, he found Margot already waiting at the entrance to the dining room. The Imperial was, as Johnny put it, the last carry-over from the regal luxury of Kaiser Wilhelm's Germany with the foyer done in red carpeting and crystal chandeliers. But he wasn't really noticing too much of the décor. It was Margot who commanded his attention. She wore an exotic orange evening gown of a soft, silky material; it was one of those low-cut affairs, revealing the richness of her smooth, creamy skin. A diamond brooch hung from her neck, contrasting the orange and tans and lighting up her face in a pale fire that turned her long hair into liquid bronze.

"You are late—the first I've known you to be," she said as he escorted her to a table behind the waiter.

As they were being seated, he said, "It's the traffic . . . tanks, trucks, the whole Russian army is in town."

"It is much the same every year at this time," she replied with some disinterest and a little irritation that he couldn't provide a better excuse. "Order me the usual, will you, darling?"

Sebastian glanced up, hoping to get some help from the waiter. It came as a shock to see Gurnt bending earnestly over an order pad, his eyebrows eagerly lifted. He looked so different in his white jacket and black tie that in the dim lighting Sebastian had to stare at him a good five seconds before being sure.

"Why don't we try something different for a change?" he asked, clearing his throat of that nervous pocket of phlegm, feeling a new sense of relief at Gurnt's being here and taking the time to run interference for him.

"The *Fräulein* would be pleased with the duck," Gurnt said simply and politely. "It is better tonight than any other time, I can assure . . ."

"Of course, the duck," she said lightly and leaned her left elbow on the table, her chin cupped in her hand. She smiled almost as if she knew he had been rescued.

"And the wine?" Gurnt added, sniffing at his pad, not looking at Sebastian now. "We have some very good Rhine wines and Bordeaux—"

"You will choose that, won't you, darling?" she prodded, her voice almost a tease, and he felt the burn on his ears.

"Oh, well, the Rhine wines will be fine," he said in an offhand manner.

"Kurt," she cut back with a rising tone of surprise now, "you know I never drink anything but Bordeaux." She leaned closer so that he smelled the light freshness of arbutus; her eyes seemed to bore right through him. "Wittenberg has put quite a veil over your memory, dear Kurt . . ."

Sebastian looked up quickly at Gurnt, who shot his eyebrows skyward. "As the lady wishes," he said, and Gurnt nodded and walked away. "You will forgive me, Margot," he added hastily, "if I seem preoccupied."

"You know I won't. I am not in the habit of being put second in any man's thinking, least of all yours, Kurt."

She took out a small compact then and began studying her lipstick in it. He knew he was feeling too tense now as he tried to play it straight with her. She was too poised, too deliberate in her sweetness, like a wife carefully laying a conversational trap to get him to contradict himself about his love affairs. The convivial atmosphere of the soft lights, white tablecloths and genuine silver, together with a six-piece orchestra, could not dispel his feeling of asphyxiation. It was her dominance crowding him and that feeling she gave him of actually possessing an extrasensory perception.

She put her compact away. "So what preoccupies you?" she went on, almost in a patronizing tone, leading him like a child.

"The Jubilee for one thing . . ."

"And?"

"Berlin being overrun with Soviet troops for another." He decided he might as well try to burrow in that direction, hoping he could find out more on the subject.

"Why should that bother you? Next Tuesday it will come and go, the parades, the show of strength for the benefit of West Berliners, the speeches. . . . It is not new to you, Kurt."

He thought she had made that statement sound like a question, and he tried the smile. "No, of course not. November seventh, is it not?"

"On my calendar it is, but I'm not sure what it says on yours," she replied dryly. Just then Willie came up with the wine and filled their glasses, put the bottle into an ice bucket on the table and left again. "We should dance," she said then, sipping her wine and watching the other couples take to the floor in the center of the room. "You are too tense, Kurt, and that makes you a bore. It is as if I am actually sitting with a bishop rather than the gay, exuberant Kurt Udal of almost two weeks ago . . ."

"I'm sorry, Margot," he returned, "it is a mood that I cannot easily shake. Every man is entitled to his moment of introspection. I regret it must be at your expense, although I am enjoying your beautiful company as always. . . . If you don't object, my feet have taken the Jubilee all day, the dancing can wait for another time . . . do you mind?"

She jerked her head to one side to indicate her indifference with that for the moment. "I take it your introspection is theological?" she prodded further, her eyes now turning on those lights of hard amusement, as they had the other night when he mentioned his spiritual vows.

"Somewhat," he replied, not pushing too far in that direction, for he had no idea how far out Udal was on the subject.

She toyed with the glass in her right hand, studying the wine for some time. "Does that mean you don't think God is the source of *Weltschmerz* any more? What about your speech to me that religion is probably for the weak people of the world who must have something to hide behind? Is that changed too?"

It could be a perfectly designed trap. To contradict it openly was to violate his Udal role. Not to contradict it was to lacerate his own self. She could be deliberately testing him—and yet she could be asking a straight question.

"Some of that I've modified," he said then. "I guess I was trying to impress you when I said it—trying to convince you that I was a good K.G.B. man . . ."

She peered at him, the wine in her glass reflecting in her luminous eyes that seemed larger in their expanded focus on him. She seemed to sense his fumbling around, because she didn't answer immediately.

"I trust you won't let Chekhov know your softening views," she said simply. "A K.G.B. man can't afford to get too bourgeois in his religious views . . ." Then, after a pause, she added, "The spirit of Luther must have hit you hard in Wittenberg, Kurt . . . you are way out of character, do you know that?"

"Not that bad, I hope," he bantered, but it fell flat against her measured appraisal of him.

"Yes . . . I'm worried about you, if you must know," she countered.

"Maybe I need a checkup . . . the glands suffer trauma at my age, so I hear."

She didn't say anything more, but kept watching him, just a trace of a smile across her eyes, her chin still resting in her hand, as if she were waiting for him to perform some magic. There was also that intentness of a cat crouching before the jump, as if she were waiting, too, to see the first unraveling of the well-knit facade Sebastian managed—so he hoped—to maintain. He tried to keep one wary feeler in her direction, the other wrapped around the significance of November 7 and the red circle on Udal's calendar. He would have to show it to Willie Gurnt—soon.

"Drink your wine," she said finally. "It will help you to relax." Just then Willie came with the duck and all the trimmings. Sebastian was glad to get busy with the meal, hoping it would help to lighten the conversation. But he had hardly gotten started when she said, "Speaking of nerves, and if that's your problem, maybe now is the time to get a good reason for them . . . here comes Colonel Chekhov . . ."

* 8 *

Run, Rabbit, Run

He would have chosen to face the whole Russian army right then rather than Colonel Chekhov. He was sure he had not yet found the proper balance with Margot, and was particularly conscious of her uneasiness with him, as if his inadequate exchanges in conversation were beginning to grate. She was continuing to play it casual, but her eyes were becoming ever more alive in their collection of his every movement, his every hesitation. He felt bound enough in her presence, but Chekhov's coming was like having all the oxygen sucked out of the room.

"You will be pardoning me this intrusion," Chekhov said, parking his German words in casual disarray. He took the extra chair Gurnt had placed at the table. Sebastian glanced at Gurnt quickly, but there was nothing in the return glance to indicate that he could do anything to poke a hole in the box that was forming. "*Fräulein*, you look like the queen of the Russian ballet," Chekhov went on in an expansive tone. His red cigarette holder bounded up and down in his jaw like a baton, chopping his words into syllables.

"Thank you, Colonel," Margot said quietly, busying herself with her food.

"And you, Herr Udal, I must confess, do not look

particularly well. . . . Is the Jubilee already that much labor perhaps?"

"It makes its demands, Colonel," Sebastian said, sawing away at his duck, glad to be diverted from Chekhov's tigerlike stare.

"Of course," Chekhov conceded with a wave of his arms, and he poured himself a glass of wine. The smile on his face was again that leer wrapped around the cigarette holder, and his monocle gleamed like the cover of a tin can in the sun, lifeless and without promise. He took a sip of the wine, then put the glass down on the table carefully. "Herr Udal, you have an American named Langley at the Jubilee . . . do you know him?" and his voice had gone curt, losing its tone of informal pleasantry, though the smile hung there like the cape of a matador hiding a sword.

The orchestra was doing something from Strauss now, and the shuffle of feet on the dance floor made a sandpaper sound to Sebastian. "There are close to nine hundred delegates at the Jubilee, Colonel," he said, continuing to chew on the duck, the meat sticking to the roof of his mouth.

"More like nine hundred and eighty to be exact, Herr Udal. It seems strange, but this man Langley is absolutely certain you are the man who would be riding with him on the bus from the western side. Does that strike you as a bit odd?"

"Quite," Sebastian replied abruptly, playing it cool, hoping for time, trying to think ahead to what action he would have to take if things got any hotter. "But I should think it would be a simple matter to prove that finally, wouldn't you?"

He could not see Willie Gurnt anywhere as he gave the room a quick glance, looking beyond Chekhov toward the dance floor. "To bring you and Langley together, yes," Chekhov agreed. "But unfortunately Herr Langley disappeared this afternoon, lifted straight out of the Jubilee before our eyes. It was a very professional job coming at a very important time—provided, that is, Herr Udal, what Mr. Langley says of you is true . . ."

"Do you think so, Colonel?"

"I am a cautious and by nature a suspicious man, Herr Udal."

"Well, does Langley know the name of the man he says he rode over here with?"

"Regrettably, no. We were preparing to show him the pictures of the Americans we have on the visa papers. By matching the names, we can easily establish the fact."

Sebastian finished his duck and dabbed at his mouth with the napkin, knowing now at least that Chekhov could not clamp irons on him yet. "Well, it is obviously a case of mistaken identity. Langley, like most Americans, is undoubtedly roaming around the city taking pictures . . ."

Chekhov did not reply, but he studied Sebastian with the intentness of a pointing Irish setter. "There is another irregularity, too," he went on. "We cannot match the ticket for the car you brought into the city with the one Wittenberg should have on you." He paused, allowing that to take effect, and then added, his voice cold now, "I am thinking, Herr Udal, that you become like the cat who thinks he walks quietly on piano keys. You will forgive me for my sense of uncertainty about you. . . . We will find Langley, and I hope that cat does not get his tail twisted, yes?"

"Just don't step on it, Colonel," Sebastian replied lightly with a smile. Chekhov stared back at him. His one good eye was green-black agate of peculiar mesmerizing power; the other eye seemed enlarged in its watery film behind the monocle.

He got up abruptly then as if a nerve had jabbed him, bowed curtly to Margot, turned and walked away, wending his way out through the crowded tables.

Margot said nothing for a long time. Her food was only half-eaten. She had taken to the wine instead, taking long gulps of it. She appeared subdued, meditative, as if Chekhov had cast a disquieting spell over her. Then, before Sebastian could open the conversation again, the room went dark and a floodlight focused on Willie Gurnt at the piano on the orchestra platform. Slowly he began to play a soft, wistful melody—and soon people began to sing along with him in hushed voices, hesitantly at first, not sure they should lose themselves in this way. Then, suddenly breaking the dam of their emotions, they let it come, and the room was filled with the words from the German favorite of the past, *"Edelweiss."*

Willie played it over again, and the crowd sang it with him, their voices completely abandoned to it now, the chorus sounding like a lamentation. He glanced at Margot. She was not singing. She sat hunched forward, that left elbow on the table, her chin cupped in her hand, the cigarette in her other. She seemed preoccupied with the song, and for the moment it seemed her face had lost its aloofness, its detachment; she was suddenly like a little girl listening to a Christmas carol, caught up in the promise of it, riding her own journey of expectation, of hope maybe, of longing perhaps. Possibly it was the wine that stripped her of her usual reticence. But she did not hasten to cover up again. And for the first time Sebastian felt a strange sense of intimacy with her, as if something were passing between them without either of them really knowing what it was. The song suddenly made him want to talk to her without constriction, without the façade, without the barrier of conflicting ideologies.

Then it ended. The lights came back on. Gurnt faded into the background. The room that had mellowed with the singing of the crowd suddenly turned hard again in its reds and yellows.

"I think I should go now," she said abruptly, suddenly aware of where she was, fumbling with her bag as if she knew she had been caught off guard.

He followed her out, wishing for some way to restrain her, not wanting to head back to his apartment now, knowing what it might mean. He hailed a cab out front, and they rode back to the rectory in silence. When they

116

arrived at the church, she said to the driver, "Wait for me." He felt some relief at that, knowing he would not have to fight her inside the rectory again, but oddly sensing some disappointment, too. And he knew that was dangerous, but the moment at the restaurant had left an effect that made it hard for him to see her other than as a human being in need of companionship like himself.

She walked to the door slowly with him, still not saying anything. He paused in the courtyard, the dim light bringing out the cobblestones and weeds. For a few seconds she seemed unsure of herself; then she put her arms on his shoulders, holding her face only a few inches from his so that he could look into those deep wells of her eyes, veiled over to prevent his seeing anything there.

"I have business at the office," she said quietly. "You will forgive me if I do not come in tonight?"

He didn't say anything, because he didn't know what would come off right. She reached up then and kissed him quickly, and he took it because there was nothing else he could do. And maybe he didn't mind, though he knew it could be the kiss of death. He might even have given it back, taken the moment, played the role to the fullest in order to feel the touch of human warmth on the surface of his own loneliness. Her mouth was warm and soft, gentle, almost shy, exploring his lips but not with feeling. And he sensed Johnny there in the shadows, smiling at him, saying, "This is the way it is, ol' buddy; you can't play this by the Book. You give and take for the Cause . . . you do what's best for the big picture and you hope God understands. If somebody gets a new lease on life, okay, you do what you have to. If you don't, you not only put the other guy on the block, but you hang yourself at the same time . . . " And he knew now what Johnny meant.

She stepped back quickly and said in a tone of detachment, "You're tired, Kurt . . . go to bed. I will see you on Thursday perhaps. By then you will have most of the Jubilee behind you . . . goodnight."

He watched her go back down the walk to the waiting

cab, her stride casual and unhurried, her movements graceful. As the cab pulled away from the front gate and moved on down the street, he saw another car across the street—a big, black one with a red star on the front door—move out to follow. He knew then what her "business" would be, she and Chekhov comparing notes. And the smell of the night was anything but a promise of a better tomorrow—it was instead the wind off the swamps that Gurnt had mentioned. He rubbed at his lips, and he wondered how much time he actually had left now.

Sebastian opened the door of the rectory and closed it behind him, reaching for the light switch. "Don't turn on the lights," the voice came to him out of the darkness. He recognized it as Gurnt's. Sebastian stood there, waiting, knowing full well that Willie's coming here only confirmed his own worst fears. He saw the drapes being pulled over the window. "All right . . . but bolt the door."

Sebastian threw the switch and at the same time slid the bolt into place. He turned to see Gurnt standing with his back to the wall by the window, his hands buried in the pockets of his black topcoat that covered the white dinner jacket.

"You made it here fast enough," Sebastian commented. "You didn't please the management by walking out on them, I'm sure."

Willie didn't answer that. He simply stood there looking at Sebastian calmly, imperturbably, as if life had no challenges. Then he took out a folded piece of paper and laid it on the desk. Sebastian walked over and picked it up. As he passed Gurnt, he smelled the strong odor of liquor. The note was done in a careless scrawl: "Meet me the same time tomorrow, same place. Mueller."

"Mueller," Sebastian said to himself, running the names through his mind. "That's Udal's contact man with the K.G.B., right?"

"Right," Gurnt said.

"Where was it?"

"Under the candlestick in the center of your table. . . . It's probably the usual dropping place for Mueller when he wants to notify you."

"How did you find it?"

"When I cleaned up your table after you left . . ."

"Does the girl know I missed it?"

Willie shrugged. "It is hard to say. She may be aware of the setup with Mueller, maybe not. It could be strictly a Chekhov arrangement."

"If she knows and noticed I didn't pick up the note, then that would explain her mood of tonight."

"The mood looked very good from where I was watching her," Gurnt countered, little flecks of amusement in his eyes. Below his eyes the pink temperature gauges showed again, a sign that the drink had raised the steam in the boiler. "You are now beginning to play like Udal, yes?"

Sebastian didn't know how to answer that without sounding childishly defensive, so he let it go. "You think she has guessed?" he asked then.

Willie shrugged in an almost disinterested way. "Perhaps. But Chekhov, I think, is beginning to see through it. The fact that he came into a strictly German-occupied restaurant to talk to you proves it."

"Yes, well, he asked about Langley . . . what did you do with him?"

Willie sniffed as if put out by being asked such a question. "He is safe in a storm drain under the cathedral . . . no one knows how to get to it except me and one trusted aide."

"If there's a way, Chekhov will find it," Sebastian countered, wishing Willie would become more alive to the dangers mounting here. "If he finds it, then what?"

"Then we will have to deal with Langley as the situation dictates," Willie retorted, and his voice was a little thick, his words just a bit slurred from the drink.

Sebastian didn't answer that one, anxious instead to tap the pulse of what was ahead.

"When and where do I meet this Mueller then?"

"Udal met him at an old bombed-out ruin where Liebknechtstrasse and Marx-Engels-Platz meet . . . there is a number, 14407."

Sebastian nodded. "What do you suppose he's after?"

Just a trace of a smile came across Willie's pencil-line mouth. "I am not a clairvoyant. Perhaps he will discuss the Genesis story of Jacob and Esau."

Sebastian smiled, then asked, "Where are we then with Chekhov and the girl? How much time do we really have?"

Willie shrugged. "It is late already," he said bluntly. "But in any case, we must wait until Sunday, yes?"

Sebastian wondered whether the forces at work now would wait that long. Finally, then, he decided to confront Gurnt with the cuff links and almanac chart. He laid them out on the desk top, not saying anything; Gurnt watched him carefully and then leaned over to study the objects, picking them up. As Sebastian disclosed his own suspicions about Richter's possession of a quarter-note cuff link and the strange tie-in of the November seventh military build-up with the quarter-moon, Willie seemed to back off.

"Coincidence," he said flatly, sniffing at it all as if it had a bad odor to it. "You are being too dramatic in your role. Anyway, you can ask Udal when you see him."

"So where is he?"

Willie shrugged. "It is not our concern now. . . . He will be on that bus Sunday; that is all we worry about."

"So I don't see him until you get me over the wall," Sebastian insisted. "I would be interested right now in how you plan to do that."

Willie did not answer. His eyes steadied on Sebastian, the pupils turning hard and black. "I am not aware of any instructions to get you out," he said shortly.

Sebastian couldn't believe it. He put both palms down on the desk and leaned on them, trying to ease his weight, which had suddenly become even more of a burden to him. "I was told you were the man who was already briefed on the job," he replied, conscious of the lameness in his voice, the fatigue, the inability to push any more, to demand. "It was Shattner's promise—"

"I have nothing to do with running people over the wall," Willie snapped. "It can't be done. My job is cover, nothing more . . . I have told them over and over again that I will not become involved with the wall—"

Sebastian lifted his hand to ward off the tirade. He had to laugh at the bizarreness of the whole thing.

"Well, you're stuck with me, Herr Gurnt," he said, dropping down into the chair. "It's a sure thing I can't get out of here myself—can I?"

Gurnt didn't answer. But his body had gone tense; his hands were jammed down hard into the pockets of his coat. "On Sunday I am through with you," he said with finality, a cutting tone in his voice. "I have told them—"

"It must be nice to be able to draw your own boundaries on life, Willie," Sebastian returned mildly.

"I have learned!" he retaliated, jerking a thumb at his chest. "It took me a long time, but I learned! You cut the length of your string by the inch, not by the yard, yes? How do you think I still have my nose on—how? Because I am not crazy like you!" Sebastian grunted his acknowledgment, because he was sensing the accuracy of that remark. "You run around like a garbage collector thinking you can clean the street by yourself! Ha! I play it like war—it is all war! Only I do not look for the medals, see? I keep my head down as long as I can—that way I don't bleed unnecessarily, yes? You give them no target, you don't die early. So—I stay away from the wall!"

It was the first time Sebastian had seen Willie lose his composure, and the drink probably had a lot to do with it. Tomorrow, he would remember—and he would not like himself. But beyond that, it was obvious that Willie had spun himself his own cocoon through a stormy, uncertain life. Sebastian sensed he was a kind of threat to that cocoon.

"Well, you are playing your job as cover well," Sebastian said then, not wanting to argue with Willie now. "You did well on the piano . . . the song was beautiful too."

Willie put his hands back into his coat pockets, and it seemed that his body sagged as the moment of eruption passed. He turned to the upright piano a few feet away and sat down to let his fingers run over the keys aimlessly.

"I played it for Fräulein Schell . . . her father's favorite," and his voice was quieter now, as if music were something personally sacrosanct. "I hoped it would make her want to leave—and it did."

"Why leave?"

"Sooner or later you were going to get into trouble in that restaurant, yes?" he said brusquely over his shoulder, as if it were unnecessary to explain it all.

"Maybe," Sebastian admitted. "Does the memory of her parents bother her that much?"

Again Willie shrugged. "All of us have a place inside like a loose domino in a stack, is that not right? Just touch it, and we move quickly to hold it in place . . ."

Sebastian nodded, a little surprised at Gurnt's discernment. "And what is yours, Willie?"

He began to pick out the haunting notes of the *Warsaw Concerto* until the melody caressed the room with peculiar velvety strokes. "I have not found it, nor has anyone else," he said over the music.

Sebastian hesitated, wanting to be careful about how he exploited the openings. "Someone knows, Willie."

He laughed in response, but it was a harsh sound, like something seldom used. "You mean God?" he said, and his shoulders shook with the chuckle. He played some more and then said, "The Jews in Warsaw," and he was referring now to the music for which the concerto was created, "they had a loose domino. . . . It was God, was it not? Hitler pulled it and the house fell in . . . all their belief of thousands of years could not keep six million of them out of the ovens . . ." He seemed to have turned it over in his mind many times before and to be asking

Sebastian for either confirmation or negation.

"Well, that domino is back very tight now in a place called Israel," Sebastian commented. Willie didn't answer. He finished the concerto and then let his fingers run again across the keys. "Why don't you try a hymn for a change?" Sebastian added, wanting to test Willie's repertoire as a kind of spiritual sounding.

"I play only what I have heard," he said shortly.

"'A Mighty Fortress Is Our God' is as German as 'Deutschland Über Alles,'" Sebastian countered.

Willie shrugged again. "The ear is attuned only to that which fits life, experience, beauty and understanding," he replied disdainfully.

So Sebastian sang the first stanza in rough style, thinking how ridiculous this was, knowing that either of them could be killed in an instant here, yet pumping sounds into the night that clashed violently with the imposed silence hanging over the land. After a minute or so, Willie began to pick out the melody with the fingers of his right hand, running it through lightly. Then, as if the exercise had become boring, he thumped a bass chord, stood up quickly and headed for the rear door. "There is only one fortress here . . . that is Ulbricht. . . . Now I go." But halfway to the door, he half turned and looked back at Sebastian, his hands jammed deep into his coat pockets again. It was a measuring look, as if checking his original computations. "You are a foolish man," he said quietly but firmly. "To come all this way just to die here for a man like Udal . . . to come without more of a plan than what Shattner gave you. . . . It is foolish . . . and a waste."

"Don't bury me yet, Willie," Sebastian said with a smile, but he knew he didn't pull it off very well, because he was thinking of that too.

Willie stood there expressing nothing, his face a clean slate. "It is inevitable," he said bluntly. And then he was gone—and the room felt empty, and the shadows seemed bigger.

The next day, Wednesday, at noon he went to 14407 on Liebknechtstrasse to meet Mueller. It was a cold, gray day with the sun sliding in and out of scuttling snow clouds. He felt nothing momentous about Mueller; he had come through so much already. He found the bombed-out ruin and climbed up into the rubble, just inside the door frame facing the street where Liebknechtstrasse and Marx-Engels-Platz meet. The sound of heavy construction equipment pummeled the shroud of bleakness, threatening to tear it open and let loose all the fury in those clouds. Now and then, when the wind shifted, he caught the faint strains of the music coming from the circus, and as he leaned his head out the door he could see the balloons bouncing in the wind beyond the line of buildings on Liebknechtstrasse.

It was nearly 12:30, and Mueller hadn't shown up. Sebastian figured he wouldn't. He was sure now that this was one of Chekhov's tests to see if he knew where to meet Mueller for the usual contact. But he continued to sit there, suddenly conscious of the boy across the square standing by the rope fence that blocked off the pedestrian traffic from the grinding, smashing construction cranes. He watched the boy alternate between sticking his cold hands into his pockets and lifting them in a kind of cheer as the cranes pounded the old buildings into gravel. Even at this distance, he knew it had to be Dettmann. The familiar blue sweater, the ragged khaki shorts, the blue stockings up to his calves—and that swagger, too, the way his body jumped with his raised fist. The sight compelled him to sit there—to ask himself why a boy would brave this kind of cold with hardly any clothes on, his body now and then hunching up against the wind, as if the construction crews needed him, as if the smoking machines would respond more because of his piercing yells or raised fist.

And suddenly he knew he would do it, only because he knew his time was running short here; if he was going to leave anything of value at all, despite the cost in the end, he would have to take whatever openings there were. So he left the bombed-out ruin at 12:30, and walked down the cement side that angled out to the right, away from the cranes, coming up behind Christian slowly and easily so as not to panic him into a run. He stood there watching him for a good minute or more, noticing how his lean body jumped when the crane smashed into the walls and sent up the shower of dust and debris. He noticed, too, the quivering in his legs and the blueness of his hands when he gripped the rope fence.

When the cranes stopped and the workmen got down to have their lunch by a barrel that gave off smoky fire, Sebastian moved up and put a hand firmly on the boy's shoulder. Dettmann jumped as if he'd been stabbed, and he tried to twist away, his terrified eyes coming around to look up at Sebastian, his head pulled down to the side, expecting a blow.

"Come with me," Sebastian said to him, still holding him by the sweater, and he pushed the boy under the rope fence, then followed. The boy stood there, head down, body quivering, maybe partly from outrage at having been found out in his private worship. "Come on," Sebastian said firmly and walked on. The boy stayed ten feet behind him, but he did not try to bolt.

When they got to where the workmen sat on planks around the smoking barrel, Sebastian asked, "Can the boy ride with one of you in the cab?" Nobody answered. They continued eating their black bread and drinking watery soup from bent tin cups. Dettmann stood forlornly off to one side, his eyes on the ground. Now and then he glanced up to see what they would do. Finally, one of the men, with a large hook nose and wide mouth that showed three teeth missing in front, waved his black bread toward the boy.

"It is against the rules, Pastor," he said.

"I will take the responsibility," Sebastian insisted. "He has been standing long enough out there. Give him a little time in the cab."

Again they said nothing, but stared at the boy, their

faces showing neither refusal nor acceptance. "Yah, the boy keeps score for us," the big-nosed man said, and this time the other three men laughed into their black bread, and Dettmann made a move to go, the laughter having cut into his pride.

"Stand still," Sebastian admonished him.

Again the big-nosed man waited, chewing slowly, not in a hurry to make the decision, eyeing Dettmann carefully. Then he shrugged, "Maybe the boy has it coming. But not long, Pastor . . . I lose my job, you know that. Let him go up into the cab there."

Perhaps this was not what Udal would have done, but it didn't matter to Sebastian. Right now the boy who hated him, the world—everything—was getting something with no price tag on it. Sebastian turned to Dettmann, who had one foot out to head back toward the rope fence, caught in the dilemma of the moment, suspicious of any favors from Udal and yet drawn irresistibly by what the workman was offering.

"Go on," Sebastian commanded him. "He said to get into the cab."

Slowly, then, Dettmann moved past Sebastian to the red crane, conscious of the men watching him. "There goes your job," one of the men said, and they laughed again, causing the boy to hesitate on the first rung of the steel ladder leading to the cab, his reddish-blue hands tightening on the step above him. Sebastian waited until the boy was safely inside before turning to walk away. He nodded his thanks to the big-nosed man, then looked up once to see the blond head just barely showing above the casing of the cab window, held stiff, straight ahead as if he were saying he was doing this only because he was ordered to. Sebastian turned to look back again when he was at the rope fence, and now the head was bobbing around as the glory of the engineering took hold of him.

He made one more check of the ruin to make sure Mueller wasn't waiting; nobody was there. Then he walked on up Liebknechtstrasse, turning to look back once as the crane motor started up, and he could see the big-nosed operator in the cab with Dettmann. He turned back into the wind, but somehow the grayness was lifting and the air felt a little warmer, even though it began to rain.

It was nearly eleven that night before Sebastian left the Jubilee. He hadn't seen Gurnt all day. There had been discussion sessions all afternoon and into the evening, and he had had to move around, finding equipment and trying to play his role as host as best he could. Today few people had confronted him; in fact, it was as if everyone knew he was not a genuine article and was deliberately avoiding him. Something was definitely changing. Faces were there he recognized; the K.G.B. were around as usual, but there was an air that hung heavy. He was in the eye of a hurricane, the first fingers of the wind beginning to pluck at him.

He didn't try to get Gurnt to take him home. It had been risky enough with him already. So he decided to walk. The night was sharp with frost. He saw the almost complete quarter-moon hanging out beyond the buildings across the street, and he thought of Udal's quarter-moon circled in fiery red. It disturbed him again as it had all day, and he wished more than ever that he could talk to someone about it, someone in the West maybe.

He walked briskly, wanting to make the three blocks as quickly as possible. He sought the anonymity of the rectory, for it was the only point of familiarity and security at this point. And the feeling of lostness was even more acute tonight as he realized that Willie Gurnt was not his ticket out of here . . . nor did he intend to be. All the bridges he had were gone. And the fact that Shattner had apparently designed it this way was ominous; there was no way to reconcile such action.

Suddenly he noticed the black car parked across the street. He was used to cars like that in the area, but as he walked, leaving it behind, he heard its motor start. And though he did not look around to check, he was certain it was creeping along slowly, keeping a few feet behind him. A sense of impending danger started somewhere along his finger tips and ran up to his heart, numbing him.

He was passing in front of the big department store, moving through the glare of the night lights in the windows, past the fixed stare of the mannequins in expensive Western tweeds and mini-skirts. And as he came to the far end, to the low fence that protected pedestrians from falling into a lot full of bricks and debris twenty feet below, he heard the car's motor speed up. He turned to look and saw the back window down and the gun barrel poking out like a broomstick. Instinctively, he went down flat on his stomach, jamming himself into the fence and trying to reach the flimsy protection of the dugout next to the walk.

The burst of the automatic weapon in the quiet, frost-hardened night sounded as if the earth itself were tearing open. The sound of breaking glass was the department store windows shattering, and the loud cracking was the bullets hitting the fence over his head. He knew that in a few seconds, as the car came abreast of him, those deadly missiles would find their mark. So he got up, kicked the rotted fence boards apart and dived through the small opening, plunging down a sickening headlong drop; and even as he went over, he felt the hammer blow across his left shoulder, telling him he had been hit. He landed, and the wind left his lungs as his body absorbed the full force of the shock.

He heard the car doors slam on the street above and jumped to his feet. He knew there was no way out now. Chekhov had apparently decided to finish it this way, the easier way, rather than trusting Udal with any more activities. Whatever the reason, Sebastian knew that he wasn't going to let it happen without giving them a run for it.

He had started across the lot full of debris when he heard the voice behind him and saw the beam of a powerful flashlight stabbing around with a long, brazen finger. He fought his way over the awkward humps of loose bricks, wire, tin cans and rusty barrels, breathing hard and coughing on the dust, feeling the numbness across his shoulder and left arm where the bullet had hit.

He came out on Rathausstrasse and ran across Spandauer Damm, heading north to Liebknechtstrasse, trying to form a plan in his mind, knowing his only chance was the U-Bahn at the Friedrichstrasse Station. He would have to check his papers on Udal to see if he had travel clearance for a train going west. He knew immediately that was impossible, since Udal could have used it long ago to go out—but he intended to try it anyway and let Chekhov work for his blood tonight.

The streets were greased with the little snow that had fallen, and the walls of the empty buildings shot off the sounds of his running footsteps like cannon into the cold night air. He should have known it would come to this finally. As he worked his laboring lungs and rubbery legs, all thoughts of Udal vanished; he was fleeing from the total monstrosity that was East Berlin now. Like Jacob fleeing Esau—only Esau was the image of Udal and Chekhov and even the Jubilee with its mockery of Christianity and the omnipresence of Ulbricht . . . even of a beautiful woman who was picking him apart with the expertness of a hawk, and of Willie Gurnt, that programed computer who played his piano like a typewriter.

And then he was on Liebknechtstrasse and running toward Marx-Engels-Platz. He saw the lights from the circus over the buildings and heard the strains of Strauss waltzes grinding through an overworked amplifying system, bravely trying to keep the day alive in people for whom the sun had gone down long ago. He heard the car squeal around the corner at the other end of Liebknechtstrasse, its headlights throwing a net of light across the darkened street, coming down to entangle him. He ran through the construction site where he had last seen Dettmann and cut around the crane that stood like a giant bug, its long neck still stretched upward, surveying the killing of the day, looking for any sign of life still there.

He ran into Unter den Linden, hoping to find a taxi, down by the City Opera Building, then dived into the shadows as the car swung into the street behind him. He stopped in back of the building and sagged against a pillar, his breathing coming in harsh sounds, almost whimpering now, while his leg muscles jumped painfully. He felt inside his suit pocket, groping frantically there as though he had lost the keys to the city—the cuff links were there, three pieces of cold metal and plastic, the poorest rationale for running, but he was going to relish the moment when he threw them down in front of Shattner and Richter. There had to be a reason for the quarter-note cuff link on Richter's sleeve. . . .

He ran a short way down Behrenstrasse, jumping from shadow to shadow, tripping over the pavement, his sense of balance upset by the pain in his shoulder. And all the time he heard the car on Unter den Linden, running up and down the street, snarling like a wasp that had had its honeycomb knocked down, hunting for it, forever hunting, refusing to accept the loss. He fell again on the sidewalk, and he wasn't sure he could get up. He felt the sticky ooze of the blood on his shirt high on his shoulder, and the night seemed to go fuzzy. Then he heard the car coming back in the quiet night, still over on Unter den Linden, but slowing to make a turn probably into Behrenstrasse. He knew then that he couldn't make it—and as he staggered to his feet, hunting for some avenue of escape, the car slid up to the curb next to him. He shrank back as the Volkswagen door flew open and a feminine voice commanded, "Hurry up, get in!"

He knew he had no choice. He piled into the front seat next to her, half falling on her. At the same instant, she threw the car into gear and they shot down Behrenstrasse. Now he could see her through the cotton blur of his pain and weakness, the black leather car coat oily from the drizzle, her hair plastered to her head as if she had been out in the rain all night.

"As the song says, 'It had to be you,'" he began, his words thick.

She didn't say anything, but concentrated instead on the driving, her eyes darting to the left and right. She came to Friedrichstrasse and swung left toward Leipzigerstrasse. "Heading for the Office of Internal Affairs, no doubt," he said, suddenly feeling warm from the heat in the car and her springlike perfume and the smell of the rain on her.

"What were you trying to do, anyway?" Her voice sounded a bit querulous.

"The trains—what else?"

"You would never have made it. You don't have the papers. Udal never did."

"All right . . . but it was better than letting Chekhov's assassins have their day. Anybody wants my blood he'll have to run a little to get it."

Again she let it go without answering directly. Then, after shifting down to cross into Gertraudenstrasse—which meant she wasn't taking him to the Ministry but back toward the general area of Alexanderplatz—she said, "The K.G.B. had nothing to do with the attempt on your life tonight."

He looked at her quickly, but she kept her eyes on the road. He waited, allowing that to sink in, to reach into his tired mind, feeling the bewilderment more than ever now, but finding it impossible to rise to its implications. "Then—who?" he asked, rubbing a hand over his eyes, trying to shake the shadows from coming across his vision, hating to pursue this any further, tired of the constricting webs of the nightmare.

"Your own people, naturally. Who else?"

He shook his head, trying to clear the fog—trying, too, to resist what she had said. He was beginning to feel the heat in the car now and those peculiar sensations across his navel, the one storm center of his that never failed to forecast accurately.

"How can you be sure—?"

"Why do you think I chased you all the way from Alexanderplatz tonight if it was Chekhov's design?" she retaliated.

"It's the cologne I'm wearing, I'm sure," he returned, and his short laugh sounded so nearly giddy that she flashed a quick look at him.

"I would have let it happen," she went on, disregarding his attempt at jocularity, "if it was a top security assignment. But as soon as I heard, I knew it had to be your people."

He half nodded, and as his head fell forward, he had the vision of huge pincers coming toward him, like those of a giant crab, while he kept blinking to shake it off. "So— now what?"

"So now I want to know why . . ."

"By yourself? What about Chekhov?"

"Chekhov would not be so gentle. . . . When he finds you it will be a long and very hard time, yes? Right now you will talk to me."

"Of course," he responded, but his own voice sounded a long way off. "Make your own scores instead of giving them to the Russians?"

And the giant pincers grabbed him by the left shoulder then, and he felt the wet leather of her coat on his cheek before they dug home. Then he sensed nothing but sweet darkness.

* 9 *

Who's on First?

He was staring at a white ceiling that looked freshly painted, and there was the smell of coffee. He looked down the length of his long body stretched out on a couch that had a bright greenish print on it; his gaze swung beyond to a large green wing chair and a love seat, and then a row of plants hanging in copper chains from the ceiling. The fireplace was deep and wide and gave off a good heat for a change. On the mantel a cuckoo clock showed it to be 3:00. How long had he been out?

His gaze stopped at her, sitting opposite him in a mustard-colored overstuffed chair, her legs drawn under her in a pose that suggested an evening of relaxation rather than confrontation. She had on that white turtle neck, and her hair was dry now and fell around her face in careless streams of gold silk. Her right elbow rested on the wing of the chair, propping her arm upward; her fingers that held the cigarette formed a "v" for victory. She watched him with the intentness of a laboratory technician.

"You like green," he said to her, trying to pierce through the too casual atmosphere.

"Color green for life," she replied dryly.

"You get no honey from wallpaper flowers; don't you know that?" he returned lightly and rose slowly to a sitting position, feeling the stiffness of the bandage on his shoulder. She didn't answer, so he added, "What day is it?"

"You have been asleep for three hours."

He paused to get a better position, then said, "Very attractive living for a sacrificing worker of the State . . ."

"We have learned to make the simple things aesthetically acceptable," she replied. He winced against the pain in his shoulder as he tried to bring the arm round in front of him. "It is not a serious wound," she said factually. "The bullet went through the fatty flesh only. . . . You lost much blood, but you will feel nothing more than a little ache. You can help yourself to some hot broth there in the pan in front of you; it will help you get your strength back . . ."

"This nourishment of tender, loving care has to be a build-up for something like twenty years at hard labor in Siberia," he said, feeling for what she had in store for him, pouring himself some of the soup and sipping it slowly. "Is it too early to ask?"

"We should start by using the English," she replied, and hearing her speak the language in a clear, crisp tone gave him a jolt, for it seemed a long time since he had heard it or used it.

"All I need now is a band playing 'The Stars and Stripes Forever' to make me cry," he returned, shifting to the English, trying to be jocular and to penetrate her carefully controlled mannerism. "Anyway, is my German so bad?"

"No, it is quite good, passable at least . . . but my English is perhaps more functional and will make it easier on you."

"Of course . . . you Communists are always one degree better at everything."

She shrugged that off and lifted her cigarette to drag on it slowly, studying him from behind the ghostly blue vapor. He sipped the soup again and then asked, "So how long have you known?"

She weighed the question for a moment, picking her

way along at her own tempo, letting him wait it out. "You did not play your role very well," she said flatly then.

"I was never good at the sleight of hand—too much of an open book perhaps," he admitted, wondering where this step-by-step word structure would lead and how much time it would take to get to the point. "When did my laundry marks start showing?"

"Perhaps not until the Imperial . . . but I was suspicious the first night. The business about theological renewal was not Udal. They should have told you that even an interview with God Himself would not have changed that man. And I checked Wittenberg before Chekhov could . . . the car you drove here was not in your name there." She picked up the yellow ticket and leaned forward to drop it on the coffee table in front of him. "There is the bill, if you want to look."

"So what kept you from turning me over to Chekhov earlier then?"

"I was willing to give you the benefit of the doubt . . . and if you were an impostor, I wanted to see where you'd lead us finally."

"And I take it Chekhov knows?"

"The best in the business couldn't fool him. But he was probably sure when Langley disappeared."

"So what was he waiting for?"

"He was waiting to see which way you'd jump, of course. . . . He was more interested in the bigger fish that had to be somewhere in the background."

Sebastian waited, thinking about that, then asked, "So what went wrong at the Imperial? Besides my ordering the wrong wine and missing the pickup from Mueller?"

"Is it so important now?"

"Well, I have some pride too . . ."

"Of course. You did not ask me to dance before dinner for one thing. Udal never missed that no matter how tired he was. But when Chekhov confronted you with Langley, everything else that showed earlier only in shadow began to take on substance . . . and, of course, the kiss . . ."

"Of course," he added lightly. "Every man's sham gets blown in sex finally, doesn't it?"

"You are not a very practiced lover," she said tartly, and he thought he saw a chip of light show in her eyes—a very faint glimmer of amusement, maybe.

"Up to now, I haven't been in the habit of kissing girls I've known only a few hours. But I catch on very fast."

"Not fast enough, I'm afraid," she countered. She pushed her legs out from under her and stood up quickly, standing by her chair, viewing him with a imperious look, her arms folded, the cigarette smoldering between her fingers like a short fuse burning down close to the powder. "You did not fool anyone, as a matter of fact," and it was as if she were anxious to point out his errors now, ticking them off for him, letting him know that she would never have allowed such cracks to show in her own performance. "There's the boy Dettmann, too—you praying in the nave at nine in the morning when Udal hardly made his regular services. And what did you think you were doing with Dettmann this afternoon, getting him into the cab of the crane as if you were giving him a free ride at a carnival?"

"I must say you cover the ground," he quipped.

"I couldn't afford to let you out of my sight, especially as I was very sure by that time that you had to be an impostor."

"Well, at least Dettmann got a taste of living," Sebastian returned, controlling his voice deliberately now, because hers was showing a sharp cutting edge.

She blew a puff of smoke from her mouth ceilingward like an exclamation point. "Yes, well what you did was reveal yourself to three of Chekhov's men watching you not more than thirty yards away across the square," she replied dourly. She began to snuff out her cigarette into an ash tray with short, killing thrusts. "An act like that in this city is bound to brand you as a Westerner—"

"I'm quite sure of that—"

"—you don't start handing out life like that in this

place," she went on, ignoring his attempt to cut in. "It is not a piece of ready exchange here that anyone accepts without serious question. Anyway, we don't need that kind of sentiment," and she began pacing short six-foot lines in front of him.

"Kids like Dettmann could use a lot more," he argued.

She ignored that and went on with, "And there's that old fool, Obenoff . . ."

"No credit references from him, I doubt," he bantered.

"Udal used him to wipe his feet on," she went on, unchecked, anxious to put it all out for him now. "Then you come in and hand him your Catechism class. When I talked to the old man yesterday, he was caught between excitement and confusion about you. He couldn't get over the fact that you didn't hang Dettmann by his thumbs after he tried to kill you with that pail of sand . . ."

"That's points for me," Sebastian injected, smiling at her, trying to interrupt the snapping recitation of her indictment.

"So the old man praises his God that the Pastor Udal has had a new touch of heaven," she half sneered. "But I know that old fool well enough by now to know that he knows the change in Udal is too drastic to be the same man." She paused then and walked over to the small, well-used coffeepot on a side table a few feet away. He watched her hand shake a little as she held the cup. She put it down quickly on the table as she finished pouring.

"So is that why you chased me tonight and brought me back here?" he asked, wanting to get to the point now. "And may I ask why you aren't turning me in to Chekhov?"

She sipped her coffee, put it down on the arm of her chair and sat down again, pulling her legs under her. Then she picked up the cup with both hands and lifted it to her mouth. "Perhaps it is that I am curious," she said.

"About what?"

"Why you have come . . . obviously you are not a spy or

trained in subterfuge. You are a total disaster in that department. And it is obvious, too, that you are too much of a clergyman—far beyond what Udal even pretended to be—to ever hope to operate in the highly disciplined, coldly detached business of espionage. So — why?"

"Well, for one, a man was in trouble; I was his only way out."

A derisive chuckle came from her—the tinkling sound of ice cubes in a glass—and he looked at her quickly. "Udal was hardly worth it—he stank of his own corruption. Didn't they tell you that?"

"A little . . . but I don't believe God stops being concerned just by the smell or even the sight of a man."

"That's a well-worn platitude. Can't you be original?"

"I don't think I can improve on Deity."

She paused to sip her coffee again, peering at him over the rim of her cup, her eyes big and luminous like the eyes of a child over a fence. "And what else?"

"A friend of mine died on the other side getting me ready for this operation. I was to be his final test in a way to see if I could make the crooked places straight."

"And?"

"I'm still bending with the curves, of course," he admitted. " 'Nothing but crooked miles in Berlin,' he said. So far he's right. Does that make you feel better, *Fräulein?*"

She didn't answer. She put the cup down on the arm of the chair. Then she found a cigarette and lighted it in slow, deliberate moves, tearing the paper match from the folder as if she were pulling a tooth.

"Anyway, you must realize by now that Udal is not even here," she went on, and he knew she was deliberately spinning the fabric to show how ludicrous his sense of mission had been in the first place. "He was probably on your side of the wall before you came here . . . he was smuggled out in Wittenberg ten days ago."

"How long have you known that?"

"In the last few hours the pieces began to fall together.

138

Your people would not have tried to kill you if Udal were still here. The question is why do they want you out of the way?"

"You've got me," he replied morosely.

"Of course," she responded triumphantly. "They obviously want Udal officially dead over here—which means they want the real Udal over on the other side to have complete freedom of movement without our counterintelligence over there getting to him. You were set up, Pastor, to put Udal in the obituary column in East Berlin." She paused for effect, allowing him to digest that juicy tidbit, then added, "So again—why? What is Kurt Udal up to over there that necessitates killing you to make him officially dead to us?"

Sebastian didn't answer. He sipped the soup, trying to total it up in his own mind. She had laid the finger on it. The cuff links and almanac chart had taken on a new dimension of relevance; he knew now that he possessed the keys to what could be a big play. And the sense of urgency to get to the West was even stronger now. Yet he knew, too, that he was caught in the vise—Chekhov hunting him down here; Shattner on the other side.

He sensed her waiting for him to answer, so he put the cup down and said, "I don't know, and that's the truth."

She kept studying him as though he were a combination lock that would open it all up for her. "So—now you have no one to rescue. Does that not bother you, since Christianity can only remain meaningful as there are people who want deliverance, yes?"

He smiled at her. "There's always you, Fräulein Schell."

She tossed her head in repudiation. Again she let go with that derisive laugh. "I am quite happy with East Berlin, Pastor," she snapped. "But it must be embarrassing for you to come all this way on a mission of mercy to find no one wants out?"

"God will provide," he teased, hoping to see her eyes pop into that snapping flame, especially now that he was being pressed into a theological corner.

She was about to speak again when there came a knock, light and careful and questioning. Sebastian tensed, then rose to his feet, looking for the exit. She went to the door and opened it, and Willie Gurnt stepped in.

For a few seconds, Gurnt just stood there taking in Sebastian's steady, incriminating gaze. Then as Margot closed the door behind him, he walked in, his hands buried in the pockets of his dark trench coat.

"They found Langley," he said, as if he were trying to formulate the rationale for being here.

"When?" Margot asked from behind him.

Gurnt half turned toward her. "About an hour ago. . . . I was with him when I heard them pulling off the grate. It must have been that *Schweinehund* helper who got paid off by them to tell. Anyway, Langley must have identified Sebastian by now. They have thrown guards around my apartment, too. . . . The K.G.B. are all over the place."

None of them said anything for a long time. Finally Sebastian asked, switching to German, "Pardon me, Willie, it's just my American habit of wanting to know who's on first. You walked in here as if Fräulein Schell were an old friend. Don't tell me you work for the K.G.B., too?"

For the first time, Willie appeared self-conscious, He shot a quick look at Margot, then strode to the fireplace, turning his back to them deliberately as if he had only now become aware of the contradiction his presence created.

"Herr Gurnt was the one who called me after the attempt on your life tonight," Margot said in a coldly factual tone, but there was a note of insistence in her voice, as if she were anxious to vindicate Gurnt.

"So how was he so sure it was I?"

"The boy, Dettmann," she replied. "He must have gone back to the crane last night. When you ran through there, he saw you. . . . He got out and ran up Alexanderplatz, not knowing whom he should tell. Fortunately, he bumped into Herr Gurnt, who got it out of him."

Sebastian stared at her, trying to keep up with the oddly shaped ingredients of this runaway night. "Dettmann?" he said half in awe. "After his trying to kill me once, I'm sure he wasn't running to get help for me."

She shrugged. "Maybe not. He might have been trying to find a Vopo and tell him where you had gone . . . who knows?"

"So Willie calls you, of all people?" Sebastian demanded, putting the question to Willie's back.

"Because he knew he couldn't get to you before Chekhov by himself." She pummeled him sharply with her words now, as if irritated that he couldn't get the picture himself.

"Considering there are West Berlin intelligence people he must know, that's a bit hard to believe . . ."

"He couldn't take a chance on hitting one of Shattner's men," she countered.

"All right, all right, but why is Chekhov so bad to fall in with at this point? Especially since you say he didn't try to knock me off tonight?"

"Time," she replied simply, and now Willie turned from the fireplace, and his face appeared white and very drawn. "He'd take too much time interrogating—"

"What's time got to do with it?" Sebastian jabbed back, but sensing now that she was closing in on the same element that hung in his own mind.

"The cuff links," Willie said then, his tired blue-gray eyes dilating in that intent way of his. He moved in closer now to stand behind her, finally feeling, perhaps, that the point of his being here had arrived.

"You laughed at me when I showed them to you last," Sebastian contradicted, still defensive about Willie's hooking up with Margot, and not knowing, either, if the two of them were deliberately trying to get evidence from him for their own purposes.

"That was before Shattner's people shot you last night," Margot continued. "Herr Gurnt felt no significance in that discovery of yours until then. . . . That's why he called me. He is sure now, as I am, that Udal is on the other side plotting something that might be disastrous for both sides of the wall." She paused, then added, "Now, may I see the cuff links, please?"

He wasn't sure of either of them. There was nothing safe here now. They could be in with Shattner for all he knew, trying to get the evidence before he could make the West. But he did not have much of an alternative. If they were Shattner's people, they could just as easily kill him right there. So he reached into his pocket, took out the cuff links and tossed them onto the coffee table. She moved over quickly and picked them up to examine them closely, probing around the shape of the musical notes. She studied the calendar and circled quarter-moon on the almanac list for November 7, then handed them back to him.

"You will have to get to the western side quickly."

"You see something in those cuff links I don't?" he asked.

"I see enough. If another man over there has a cuff link that matches these," and she frowned now, "then it cannot be by accident . . . not just one link as you have told Herr Gurnt."

"All right, then, it should be easy enough for you to arrange transportation to the other side," Sebastian suggested.

She snorted and lit another cigarette, and Willie turned back to the fire as if the cold of the night were beginning to get to him. "I am not K.G.B., nor do I have access to transportation permits through the wall. . . . Even if I did, if you land over there so easily, you can be sure the Gehlen Bureau or the Allied Command would suspect you as a plant by us. . . . It would take too much time convincing them."

"Then you think it all has something to do with November seventh and the Russian troops being here?" he probed.

She shrugged. "Who knows? It may not be anything at all. But we can't afford to think there won't be something involved like that."

"Any kind of incident at the wall with all this Russian military here," Willie cut in blandly, "could spark something too big for either side to handle."

"I didn't know you cared, Willie," Sebastian countered.

"He doesn't," Margot cut in. "It's his job at stake if anything blows up."

"What job has he got left now that Chekhov knows—and now that you know?"

"He can defect to East German Intelligence—that way Chekhov can't touch him."

"You don't care which side you're on, Willie?" Sebastian asked.

Willie's quick, lifeless smile was no more than a nerve jumping in his upper lip. "The side that pays," he said with a shrug and turned back to the fire again.

"Just so you get to play the piano, right?" Sebastian tried jogging him, but Willie didn't respond. Margot had one eyebrow lifted as if to say that was the reality of things here. "Well, you have courier service; why don't you notify Western Intelligence on the other side that you figure maybe Shattner's got Udal up to no good over there?" he asked her.

"Only Chekhov can clear that," she said with finality. "And since the evidence so far is rather flimsy at best, Chekhov won't risk his reputation to use the red phone to the West. It will take too much time for Chekhov to make up his mind—that is the Russian nature. And even if they got the word on your side, they would go slow with Shattner without more positive proof."

"So what you're saying is that I've got to go over there and drop in on Western Intelligence before Shattner knows I'm there—and hope they don't laugh in my face?" Neither of them answered him, their silence indication enough that this was the only way and the most difficult

143

of all. "What do I do, then, pole-vault the wall?" he continued, growing impatient now with the whole business.

A smile came across her lips. "You need a miracle," she said lightly in a kind of left-handed jab at his faith.

"Okay, just so I know what to order," he returned, seeking to match her banter.

"There isn't much to plan on," she said then factually. "I will check the possibilities for going out but there won't be anything before Saturday, if then."

"In the meantime, where do I hang my hat? Chekhov is poking every shadow for me, and Shattner's gang—if it's they—are waiting for another crack at me, no doubt."

"You will go to the place I have arranged with Herr Gurnt . . . I think I should drive you there now before it gets daylight. You should stay there; do not go out or reveal yourself—understand?"

Sebastian nodded and she pulled on her car coat, heading for the back entrance. She drove them in her Volkswagen, winding around back streets where the K.G.B. probably would not be patrolling. Sebastian noted the various street signs, trying to orient himself with them—Spittelmarkt, Niederwallstrasse, across Unter den Linden and into Clara-Zetkin-Strasse. She turned finally into a short street that had only a few old ruins and shot the Volkswagen into a narrow passageway.

"Quickly," she said as they got out. "I will be here on Saturday evening." She backed the car out into the street and was gone.

"I get the feeling she takes too many risks for what she gets back," Sebastian commented to Willie as they watched her go. "How can you be sure of her?"

"I am sure of no one," Willie replied flatly. "I measure each step before I take it, yes?"

They were standing by an old, two-story, rambling structure of red brick that was chipped and scarred, and leaned dangerously to the left like an old man standing on one leg.

"Why here?" Sebastian asked.

"Used to be an old munitions supply depot," Willie explained. "You see the driveway going down to the basement loading platform through those doors . . ."

"That doesn't answer my question," Sebastian prodded.

"All right then—you see that there?" And Willie pointed to the bright, luminous green lettering on the wall above their heads:

VERBOTEN—SPRENGSTOF!

"Explosives?" Sebastian said, not comprehending, but Willie was already going up the steps to the scarred front door. They walked through the door and into a damp main room. There were little cubicles here and there off to the side that must have been offices at one time. The building smelled of the usual decay—and oddly enough the sharp tang of German sausage.

"There," Willie said, indicating the stairway going down. Sebastian moved over to it and saw the jagged hole in the steps and the long, cylindrical, rusted bomb hanging out.

"A bomb?" Sebastian gasped, for it wasn't exactly what he had in mind for companionship the next three days.

"A delayed-action incendiary from the war," Willie explained. "They shut off the time mechanism long ago, but the demolition people have not been here yet. That is why the building still stands."

"Can it still go off?"

"If the timing device is reactivated inside, perhaps.
. . . They put a cotter pin on the top a long time ago to hold back the gear."

"And if I pull the pin?"

"Maybe you prove something then, yes?" Willie replied with a sniff. "Anyway, it will keep the Vopos and the

K.G.B. from checking in here—they won't suspect anyone of taking the chance of sitting on a bomb."

They moved back into the main section with its sausage
odor, and Sebastian was turning to ask Willie if he could
smell it when he observed a shadowy shape moving toward them from the far end of the long room.

"Who is that?" Willie asked sharply.

The shadow stopped, suspended before them. They all
stood still for what seemed a long time before a voice,
rather tremulous, said, "It is only I, Herr Gurnt, Obenoff
. . ."

Sebastian and Gurnt, both anxious to know the meaning of the old man's presence here, moved quickly to him
until they could make out his face in the dark. The smell
of sausage was stronger now. Willie flicked the beam
of his flashlight around. They were there, all five of them,
sitting like birds on a clothesline and clutching brown
paper sacks in their laps. Sebastian now knew the source
of the smell—those bags were probably full of sausage
sandwiches. The beam moved quickly to the old man
sitting on a packing crate opposite them; he was decked
out in a black suit and black bow tie, had a black fedora
perched squarely on his head, and was clutching a
wooden case close to his chest.

Willie turned off the flashlight, and they stood in the
darkness again. Nobody said anything, and it was as if
nobody wanted to. Finally Willie said, "Obenoff, you
can't stay here with them . . . we are not waiting for any
train to the West."

But even before Willie said it, Sebastian knew Obenoff
was not going to yield easily, if at all. He heard a paper bag
rattling in the dark, then the sound of someone's jaws
working over the bread. Sebastian caught Willie's eyes in
the dim half-glow, and there was a look both of indignation and helplessness. Now was not the time to argue, the
Germans would say, when someone was eating.

146

* 10 *
A Company
of Impossibles

They stood in the center of the room while the boys went on eating their black-bread sandwiches. Only thin slivers of light came in the back windows from a solitary lamppost beyond the empty lot to the rear of the building, casting a kind of dusty pallor over them. Obenoff shared a thermos of coffee with Sebastian and the other man who, Sebastian was sure, was the same one he had seen earlier that week in the church.

Willie refused to accept any coffee; he stood against the wall a few feet away, his arms folded in a pose of truculence. "You cannot stay here," he repeated several times to Obenoff.

Obenoff was intent on explaining it all to Sebastian, but only after he had introduced the other man, who had stepped up close now, still clutching the box to his chest. "This is Otto Kubeksten," Obenoff said. "He worked for the circus in the balloons. . . . The K.G.B. took his job away . . . something about his past political associations."

"I am a diamond cutter, a member of the Kubeksten cutters, the most famous in Europe," Kubeksten threw in eagerly. He clutched the box tighter; it obviously contained cutting tools as precious to him as the family jewels. "They want me to feed the animals . . . me, who once cut diamonds for the royalty of Europe," and his voice carried a wounded tone. His deep-set brown eyes were watering, and his nose ran.

"You should be thankful you have a job," Willie snipped at him morosely.

"There are some things an artist should not do," Kubeksten protested, to which Willie only gave a grunt.

"Herr Kubeksten is not well," Obenoff continued. "His heart . . . the work of feeding tigers could kill him . . . his only chance is to the West."

"You think you can get over the wall with a bad heart?" Willie countered again. "Anyway, how did you know we were here?"

Obenoff glanced at Willie, but when he spoke, it was to Sebastian. "I did not know for sure," he began. "When Dettmann told me about the shooting last night, I knew your time here was short. I knew then that if it was possible at all, the boys should go out with you . . . and Kubeksten. . . . I did not know how to make the contact, but there were two places Herr Udal would go now and then to meet other men. . . . One was at Marx-Engels-Platz at the old ruin there. The other was here. I didn't think you would go to the old place, since it was so open; so I decided to try this place, praying you might know of it too, and come here to hide until you decided to go."

Obenoff kept his tired gray eyes on Sebastian's face, looking for a sign that would tell him it was all right. Sebastian turned to look at the boys again, sitting on the long bench, their hands dipping into the paper sacks, intent on the pleasure of the moment—one they apparently rarely had. Only Dettmann, perched at the far end, was not eating, his ever-watchful face partly hidden in the darkness.

"Do they want to go, Herr Obenoff, or are you sending them?" Sebastian asked.

"Well, after the shooting was over," Obenoff responded, leaning into it now with some sense of excitement that Sebastian was not turning him aside, "Dettmann comes back to the church and tells me what happened . . . then he asks me directly if Herr Udal is really Herr Udal, you see? So I tell him," and Obenoff seemed embarrassed now, "that I think perhaps the Udal we have known this past week is someone who looks like the other Udal only, yes? So Dettmann leaves me and comes back later with the other boys . . . they talked together, he said, and if the new Udal is from West Berlin, they would like to go if the new Udal would have them."

"There is nothing any better for them over there," Willie cut in again in a petulant tone.

"Boys their age should have a warm bed at night and be able to open their eyes once to a day that can offer something of life," Obenoff replied with some vehemence. "Anyway, there is nothing here for them now but a life of wandering and being tortured by some other worker of the State."

"It is no place for children," Kubeksten added sadly.

"But Herr Sebastian has no room for baggage," Willie insisted.

Obenoff looked at Willie over his bent glasses, then turned his eyes slowly back to Sebastian, waiting, the look of fear returning slowly in his old wrinkled face. He looked forlorn suddenly. His gray hair stood in tufts on his head like lumps of cotton and his skinny neck poked out of the oversized white collar, making the body look as if it didn't match the head. There was frailty there, a result of the inner torment experienced by a true man of God in a community that scorned his presence. But there was resilience too—in the jawline, in tired eyes that could flash sparks of indignation.

"Herr Gurnt is right," Sebastian said quietly, not wanting to destroy too quickly the hope that burned in that face. "I have no plan to go over the wall. There is only one flimsy chance that I might get a special courier on Sunday. If that does not come through, then I am a prisoner here. And unless God provides some way out, I can't help you—or them—or Herr Kubeksten."

The rattling of the paper bags by eager hands suddenly

quieted. Kubeksten heaved a long, tremulous sigh, gulping air, his Adam's apple bouncing like a ping-pong ball in the tight stocking of his neck.

"But allow them to remain with you anyway," Obenoff asked. "Let them experience the hope for a while—is that asking too much?"

"You want them to sit on a bomb?" Willie demanded again. "You want them to be caught here? What happens to them then?"

"What have they been sitting on for most of their short lives?" Obenoff returned, trying to put the indignation he felt into his mild spirit. "They have never hoped for anything better—yet this is their only chance. Give them that at least!"

"They can stay," Sebastian said then.

Obenoff bowed his head and rubbed a shaky hand across his scrubby gray hair, a sign of the relief he felt. But Willie moved away from the wall and walked into the front room, wanting nothing more to do with them.

"Now I must go," Obenoff said, taking Sebastian's hand in his.

"You are welcome to share in the hope—with them," Sebastian said.

Obenoff shook his head. "There is the church. There are not many who come now, but someone should be there." He paused then, sorting out his words carefully, for he was not a loquacious man. "I do not understand why you did this thing, to become Udal, but a true man of God cannot hide the light. Some always shows through. You have not failed because of that . . ." He wanted to say more, but his mouth could only work over the words that would not form. "So . . . *auf Wiedersehen!*"

He turned and embraced Kubeksten, then hugged each of the boys one by one. As he turned to leave, tears streaked down the dry, leathery skin of his cheeks. "Do not eat all your sandwiches at once," he said to them. "I have put blankets for you in the bag there. Fritz, there is a little medicine in the bag for your cough. Christian, you

lead them now, make them obey . . . and trust God. . . .
Auf Wiedersehen and God be with you, *Liebchen!*"

Willie let him out the front door, and Sebastian moved
to the window with the broken glass to watch the old man
wander up the deserted street, pulling his bulky overcoat
around his thin frame, holding onto his battered black hat
against the early morning breeze.

"You could not even fool the old man," Willie commented from behind him.

"Least of all him," Sebastian replied, watching him
disappear around the corner at the far end of the street.
"It is said that old men and children have the best eyes
and ears to detect contradictions."

Willie sniffed at that and added, "It is a cruelty to hold
out hope for them and destroy it so quickly . . ."

Sebastian didn't bother answering that. He didn't know
how to right then. His shoulder throbbed continually now,
and he felt tired. It was cold and damp in the building that
rattled under the wind. He didn't want to think of the
others right then. Willie was articulating his own sense of
futility. It would be harder with the boys here, harder to
plan, harder to make it out. But right now they had their
hope, and he decided to let them enjoy it.

"We'd better find a place so we won't be seen," he said
to Willie finally. "It will be a long three days . . ."

They couldn't do much during the day for fear of attract-
ing attention. Sebastian made the boys stay in their blankets in an inner room that had no windows. For a time
they accepted this, but the long hours brought a tedium
that finally erupted in serious fighting. The grunts and
screams and bellows echoed through the cavernous building, threatening to alert anyone for blocks. When Gurnt
finally threatened to return them to the church, they
quieted down and took to playing simple games that
Sebastian designed for them. All this time Kubeksten sat
on his packing crate in the big room as if he were waiting
for a bus, holding that mahogany-colored box close. Now

and then he dozed, and his head fell forward so that the fedora dropped off his head and rolled across the floor.

At night, Sebastian and Willie had to find ways to entertain the boys. They caught on to hopscotch quickly, and the only sounds at night were the muffled thumping of stocking feet hopping the squares and the restrained laughs as someone failed in the process—especially if it was Gurnt, whose attempts were comical at best.

Only Dettmann stayed outside the fun. He leaned against the far wall, his arms folded over his faded blue sweater, and glowered at his companions. Sebastian watched him, wondering what the boy was thinking, trying to find some point of contact. But Dettmann was not allowing himself to get close enough to Sebastian; the scars from Udal had left him distrustful.

At dawn, Sebastian would order them into their blankets again on the stone floor of the inner room, allowing them to munch on the few remaining sandwiches. Once he read the story of Joshua at Jericho from his worn pocket Bible, and when he finished young Fritz raised his head off the floor and peered at Sebastian with large, brown eyes.

"Herr Sebastian, is that the way you will lead us out?" he asked, his voice pitched high in the wonder of the moment.

There was a minute of silence, and the other four heads lifted as one to look at him, waiting for the answer. "How's that, Fritz?"

"Will you pull the wall down like Joshua, blowing horns and marching around it?"

Sebastian hesitated, wondering how much he could actually promise them in the name of God in this situation. "Well, Fritz," he said finally, "I don't know what God has in mind, but I suppose if He wants to do it that way, He can."

"*Himmel,*" Fritz replied, dropping his head back onto the floor, "wouldn't that shake up Ulbricht?"

And then someone giggled under the blankets, and it

took a while for them to quiet down. But when they did, they lay staring up into the pale light, wondering whether they would actually go out at all.

As darkness fell—after a full day of watching the military traffic and the black K.G.B. cars pass the old ruin—Sebastian and Willie went up onto the roof to get fresh air and to survey the scene. They could see the lights in West Berlin clearly enough, winking their promise of something better.

"Over there," Willie began, pointing his finger toward the shroud of darkness, "is the Brandenburg Gate—not more than half a kilometer. But it might as well be a hundred as far as those kids and the old man are concerned."

Willie's voice carried a note as if the situation were beginning to demand too much of him.

"There's always hope, Willie," Sebastian said, trying to inject some optimism.

"Hope will not give you wings," Willie returned sullenly. "I said it was cruel to build hopes. Now you see what I mean. It will be worse for them now to have to go back after they have had these few hours to think about it. They have come to know the luxury of one relaxed moment. They smell the promise of the journey, a journey that will never come. And the old man sits down there with his tools, just as sure as if he were going to be picked up by all the royalty of Europe and carried away to a ready-made diamond-cutting business."

"You sound as if they are beginning to mean something to you, Willie," Sebastian said mildly.

"Even I will not hold out meat to a dog and then kick him in the tail," Willie snapped.

Sebastian sensed the truth of that. "So maybe there is a way," he tried again, stubbornly clinging to the hope.

He saw Willie's quick glance at him in the dark. "I said before I would not get involved with the wall. You cannot win against it. No one has bothered trying for a long time now. To try it, I am as good as dead—dead if I try going over, dead if I fail. So it means nothing to me finally what happens to them . . ."

"What man makes, God can unmake," Sebastian commented.

Willie grunted his disdain for that. "Only an idealist thinks like that here. . . . Here we are realists; we know the odds, and we don't see many tracks of God in this place. We have the Udals only, who have tried to coax God in here, but in the end have wound up themselves to be infidels. And even you—you come for God and your own people try to kill you. How can you hold onto a God that crumbles like that in your hands?"

There it was—the familiar jab of a man trying to make up for personal suffering by anti-God invective. So Sebastian was coming close to Willie's "loose domino."

"God never gave *me* any blank checks, Willie," Sebastian returned. "I draw only on what I have. Sometimes it's pretty lean, the supply of miracles; sometimes they even come from people I least expect. Sometimes there aren't any. I sweat it out and keep trying the doors; some I even kick in when necessary. And since I'm no operator like you, when things happen, I figure it has to be God . . . understand?"

Willie only sniffed in the dark and kept staring out at the lights.

"Anyway," he said finally, not wanting to pursue it any further, fearing the truth maybe, "you will not read any more about these Joshuas to them . . ."

He left then, and went back down the stairs. Sebastian stayed on the roof a long time, hunched up against the cold, watching the lights, praying that something might materialize. His tired mind groped for a design, some vague shape of an idea that might work—but after a while, he realized that it would all depend on Margot Schell. If she got him on the courier's jeep tomorrow, then he'd almost have to accept, because the larger picture demanded it. But could he leave five kids and an old man behind? Now, as he thought of them, he wondered how quickly the choice had materialized—those five boys and old Kubeksten showing up when they did. And old Obenoff coming to this place just as if he knew exactly how the whole thing would shape up.

But he hadn't much time for further consideration, because he saw Margot Schell below, coming across the empty lot from the rear. He went downstairs quickly while Willie let her in the back door. She flicked a quick glance at Kubeksten, then at the boys, who were sitting on that long bench with their blankets rolled up under their arms, each of them looking rather frail and lost, watching her closely, for they sensed she held their sentence now.

But she ignored them, as if maybe she half expected them to be there. She joined Willie and Sebastian in the center of the room, Kubeksten having gone back to his packing case where he seemed to be holding down the lid on seven demons that threatened the groaning old building.

"I could not get a way clear for you," she said, jamming her hands down into the pockets of her black leather car coat. "I tried . . . but the contacts I had inside the Ministry, who might have worked up the necessary papers, won't do it now that Chekhov is breathing fire."

Nobody said anything. One of the boys behind Sebastian sniffed loudly, and Fritz started to cough, trying to cover it with his hand. A long, shaky sigh came from Kubeksten.

"What are your suggestions then?" Sebastian asked, his own voice sounding hollow here in the empty room.

"Some other way, of course. Or maybe the best thing to do is to go back to Chekhov with the story about Udal and hope he goes for it enough to alert the other side." She didn't sound convinced about it, however, and he thought he detected a testy note in her voice now, as if she had been over it a hundred times since he had last seen her.

"What are the odds on that?" Sebastian prodded. "Fifty-fifty?"

"Ten to one against," Willie cut in abruptly. "Chekhov is as mad as a horse with a wasp biting his rump by now—he'll make you sweat a long time before he listens to anything as fancy as three cuff links and an almanac chart."

Kubeksten got halfway off the packing box then as if he wanted desperately to say something, then dropped back as she glanced at him. Again there was a long pause, and Sebastian felt them waiting for him.

"The man of God is thinking of blowing horns around the wall?" Willie said sardonically.

Sebastian didn't respond. He was watching Kubeksten now, who kept rocking on that packing case, his mournful eyes peering up toward Margot expectantly as if he were waiting for the cue. And then Margot's eyes merely flicked over him as a kind of nod to him, and the old man got up ponderously, almost shakily, and stood there clutching his toolbox like an old war veteran responding to his last muster.

It was at that moment, while Kubeksten stood there swaying like a clown on stilts and clearing his throat for what he had to say, that Sebastian saw it all in one quick shutter-clicking connection in his mind. It had all been set up by her in just this exact way. There could be no other explanation for it. His nagging doubts about old Obenoff's suddenly appearing here with five kids at that precise moment to wait it out on a live bomb were not fanciful now. Even the whole sense of disbalance he had about Willie Gurnt's coming over on her side just on the business of the cuff links was not a myth, either. She had found out about Willie some time after the night at the Imperial—maybe when she traced who picked up Mueller's note—and had gotten to him, and bought him out for herself just to make sure, probably, that Sebastian was indeed the religious sentimentalist she needed to go the whole way here. She had never intended to get him out by courier, either, or even through Chekhov; whatever importance she had placed on the mystery of the cuff links had taken second place to the other thing that was driving her.

And now Kubeksten. This old man, who was as out of place as a blackbird in a wren party, had been invited here by her for one purpose: He had the one means that could be used in the attempt to go over the wall. As ludicrous and suicidal as the idea was, it was but symptomatic of her desperation to balance the books for what she had done to her parents a long time ago. He couldn't be sure of this, of course, but nothing else made sense. She had to find expiation for her guilt—and what better way than to engineer the means to get a minister, five kids and an old circus clown over the wall? That could go a long way toward easing her tortured conscience.

And as he stood there peering at her steadily, entranced for the moment by the bordering madness that drove her, he wanted to confront her with her perfidy. She stood there coolly in her controlled mask of innocence, manipulating them cleverly along the string of her carefully thought-out plan, apparently unmindful of the terrible destruction she was plotting for them all. But he knew he wouldn't confront her—whatever terrible agony seared her inner self in what she was doing was probably enough as it was. To expose her in front of the others would only demean her perhaps beyond herself; in it all, he was still peculiarly sensitive to her as a person, still strangely drawn to that part of her that ran on a different circuit than the hard, scheming, emotionless exterior.

"Well, old man, do you crow or weep?" Willie snapped impatiently as Kubeksten continued to stand there clearing his throat and darting uncertain glances at Margot.

"There—there is a way," Kubeksten finally said, heaving that shaky sigh. He waited again, clutching the toolbox closer to his chest, and then said, "There are the balloons . . ."

In the silence that followed, Sebastian saw Margot's eyes dart just once in his direction, as if trying to see his reaction to what Kubeksten had said. He knew then that she wasn't going to decide on that finally; she was going to let Sebastian do it. She didn't want to be the one responsible for the final commitment to the mad plan, for if it failed she would have ten times more of a burden to carry. And she had to know, too, that he wouldn't dismiss it so easily, either; she had to know now that as a minister of his particular stripe, he would examine it all carefully in the light of the human factors here.

"Tell us another joke, old man," Willie finally said, his voice carrying a growl of disgust. And when nobody said anything to that, he laughed in an explosive sound of ridicule. "You people *are* crazy! Do you have any idea how hard it is to get a balloon like that into the air?"

"Kubeksten says it can be done," Margot said flatly then.

"Ha!" Willie countered. "This old man, once he gets launched, won't be worrying about five children—"

"Then let me try it, but spare them," Sebastian offered finally.

"That's impossible now," she replied with finality.

"Why?"

"Chekhov picked up Obenoff last night," and her voice had gone quieter, the note of exhaustion creeping in. "The old man will try to hold out to the last before he talks, but Chekhov knows the boys have probably hooked up with you to go out. That makes them enemies of the State."

Silence again. The kind that moved in on people who were up against the wall now and had very few options. She had stitched it together very neatly, Sebastian thought, sealing off any possible alternatives. So Sebastian said finally, "Well, it's better than Joshua with the horns, Willie," trying for the lighter vein in the gloom that had descended on them. But even as Willie snorted his disdain for that, Sebastian couldn't help but wonder if he could allow himself to tempt God beyond his prerogatives in consenting to a scheme like this.

* 11 *

The Desperate Hours

Willie argued it out doggedly for a long time, because it demanded of him an involvement far beyond what he was willing to accept. And the more he talked, the more Kubeksten became nervous about it. But finally Margot told Willie to shut up or go on back to his piano playing. It stopped Willie long enough for Sebastian to ask, "Herr Kubeksten, why don't you tell us what you have in mind?"

"Murder, that's what," Willie cut in flatly. "You won't be flying monkeys in those balloons, old man, it'll be five kids—"

"Let him talk, Willie," Sebastian urged.

Kubeksten sniffed loudly and nervously, lifting one hand to touch his fedora before he spoke. "There are seven smaller balloons, three big ones," he began. "The big ones take twenty-five hundred cubic feet of hydrogen, big enough to carry a man up to a hundred and seventy pounds. The smaller ones take fourteen hundred cubic feet and maybe carry one hundred pounds. That's barely enough for the boys."

"So how do you expect to get those balloons out from under the circus?" Willie demanded again. "And how do you intend to fill balloons here with highly dangerous gas practically under the noses of the Grepos on the wall and the K.G.B. prowling all over town?"

"One question at a time," Margot snapped at him.

"It is my responsibility to pack the balloons for storage now that the season is passed," Kubeksten went on. "I am supposed to do that tomorrow night. . . . I can drive the truck here. . . . The hydrogen is stored in the big tank on the truck . . ."

"So you will park the big truck out front as if you were delivering milk?" Willie cut in again.

"He'll drive it into the loading dock area below here," Margot answered, for she had this all figured out.

"Then we can run the hundred feet of coupling feed pipe from the truck up to the roof," Kubeksten went on, taking courage from Margot's assistance. "It takes only thirty minutes to fill the big balloons, maybe less for the others. . . . In the dark no one should see—"

"The dark," Willie scoffed. "It's hard enough to get those things up in the daylight when you can see what you're doing. What about weather? And things like ballast? I know enough about this business that you don't just suddenly launch a balloon without a lot of instruction . . . unless you want to commit suicide, is that it, old man?"

Kubeksten sniffed again, and his eyes in the dim glow lifted to them like a dog's eyes appealing for understanding.

"It is true," he said lamely. "The cold weather is not good . . . we need warmer air to rise quickly—"

"Monday promises to be warmer, up to sixty," Margot chimed in then. "Will that do it?"

"It will do," Kubeksten returned.

"Until Monday," Willie scoffed. "The K.G.B. all over the place now, and you think we can wait till Monday? What happens to our friend Sebastian's mission to get to the right people over there before the seventh?"

"You are not helping matters any by your arguments," Margot retaliated.

"On the contrary," Willie shot back, "I'm doing you the favor of poking the holes in this thing before you get them a few hundred feet off the ground, yes?"

"Let's come to the point," Sebastian jumped in, for he knew that the temperature was going up all the time they argued, and it wasn't helping Kubeksten, who probably wasn't too sure of all this anyway. "If our chances are better of going over on a warmer night, then we'd better hold to it—there's no point in trying against percentages that say we won't have much chance. We'll take the time here and hope for the best. . . . Now, Mr. Kubeksten, can you teach us how to handle these balloons?"

Kubeksten took his time now, clearing his throat several times and sniffing, trying to find a comfortable place on that packing case.

"It takes me four months to learn," he began, laying out the precariousness of what he was being asked to do. "A balloon is not something easy to control. . . . There is wind, temperature . . . but you must know when you unload ballast, when to pull the valve that sends you down to earth. Even for me, I have sailed a balloon always anchored to the ground. Once only did I try without. It was a rough day and dangerous, so I cannot say it was enjoyable. You must always watch for landing on electric lines . . . you must not descend too quickly, or you can smash yourself to pulp. . . . And in the dark, it is more difficult, yes?"

Nobody said anything, not even Willie. Kubeksten's recitation of the problems fell on them with peculiar subduing power. "Herr Kubeksten," Sebastian finally cut through the momentary lull, "we have only a half-kilometer to go . . . does it demand great skill to go that far?"

"The skill is in getting off the ground and landing again," Kubeksten returned almost dismally. "Distance means nothing."

"You will have to teach us all you know in the next few hours before daylight and before you must go back to the circus," Margot cut in then, dismissing the former options. "There is no choice in the matter. It is all a question of how much you want to start cutting diamonds again,

Herr Kubeksten. . . . There is no longer any hope for you here, or for them." She nodded to the boys still sitting there quietly on the bench, caught in the wonder of what was unfolding before them.

As Kubeksten looked from her to the boys, it seemed his face sagged even more in the pale light. But he nodded slowly, yielding to the facts.

"Count me out," Willie said with finality. "I'm not going to be a part of sending seven people to that kind of death . . ."

"I am afraid we will need you, Herr Gurnt," Kubeksten returned quickly. "To launch the larger balloons alone will take all the hands we have . . . already we are too few."

"It can't be done, don't you see?" Willie insisted.

"It will be like hopscotch, like one big hop, yes, Herr Gurnt?" came another voice then, jarring the flow of the exchange, and the innocence and eagerness of it left them groping for an answer.

They waited for Willie to reply. But nothing came. It was one thing for Willie to fight off Kubeksten and the others, quite another to squirm out of a boy's entreaty. Especially Fritz. For Willie had dropped his guard before Fritz during the long hours of hopscotch—and there had emerged that peculiar affinity of two spirits.

"Well, Willie?" Sebastian prodded, noting how Willie had tried opening his mouth several times to answer.

"The boy does not understand that this is not a game," he said finally, but it did not come off with any conviction.

They waited in the silence that was getting awkward until Margot broke in impatiently. "We should go downstairs where Kubeksten can work by the light."

No more was said. One by one they filed down the steps, moving carefully over the bomb as if it were a tiger sleeping in the dark. Glancing back, Sebastian noticed that Willie had remained behind. He thought maybe he would say something to encourage him, but then he realized it was Willie's moment to ponder now—to make his decision—and anything said to him could only add to his stress.

For three hours, Kubeksten did his best to prepare them for what was ahead with the balloons. The loading-dock area where they worked was littered with debris and sealed as tightly as a tomb, except for one ventilating hole high in the wall. They found an old mahogany table top, and spread it over two crates for Kubeksten to work on. Then, by the light of the flashlight, he worked up the diagrams of the balloons on the back of a circus program with an old ball-point pen. Carefully he illustrated each part—the descent valve, the rip panel cord, the ten ropes attached from the net to the basket ring, the bags of sand ballast attached to the basket (very important, yes?); then on to the particulars of the flight, Kubeksten's pen making slashing, nervous lines. "Never unload too much ballast to go up, or you go too high, maybe beyond the clouds to where there is no oxygen . . . never pull the descent valve too soon to go down . . . if you are too high, you will hit hard—and kaput! You want to descend slow, then you use the descent valve in short jerks, yes? And never pull the rip valve that lets all the air out until you are sure you are on the ground . . . if you do, it collapses and you are dead again, yes?"

Sometime during all the intense explaining, Willie joined them in the background. Nobody looked up except Fritz, whose brown, fawnlike eyes rose in expectancy.

They went over the diagram again and again, and Kubeksten quizzed the boys especially about all he had said; only Dettmann shrugged off the questions, his arms folded in that pose that said he was beyond all that. The instruction went on until the first light filtered through the circular vent holes. By then the air had become stale with their breathing and sweating. They had asked a lot of questions. Margot asked about the direction they would go and how and where they would land. It depended on the wind, Kubeksten replied, but it would be best to aim for the Brandenburg Gate and the woody Tiergarten east. And if the wind was wrong?

"So," Kubeksten said with a shrug, "we could land in Yugoslavia, maybe back to Russia—wind is something you cannot control, yes?"

"Can we get high enough to be out of the lights of the wall so the Grepos don't see us?" Sebastian asked.

Again Kubeksten's sweaty forehead crinkled up. "If the balloon goes up good to start, you can rise three hundred feet in a half-kilometer. If it drags low to the ground, sometimes it never goes up more than fifty feet in ten miles. Then you must ballast wisely, yes? You throw enough out to get up, not too much to go too high."

And when it ended, finally, with Kubeksten pulling on his old black overcoat for the ride back to the circus with Margot, there was still no real sense of confidence in the room. If anything, tension seemed to be mounting. It was written in Kubeksten's preoccupied stare as if he were already seeing the disaster ahead. It was there in Willie, who looked even more dubious, that scythe-shaped hairlock hooked down over his right eye as though mocking the absurdity of it all. It was in Margot, too, as she stood a few minutes with Kubeksten waiting, a burning cigarette to her lips, eyes fixed on that scratched-up worksheet. Only the boys viewed it with a carnival spirit, walled off from any visions of disaster by the adventuresome spirit of youth. It was hard to quiet them in their blankets as the dirty, gray light of another rainy day seeped into the inner rooms. But finally their tired bodies succumbed. Willie sat up against the wall with his knees drawn up. Sebastian sat a few feet away and turned it over in his mind again and again—finally he sought peace in prayer as his body ached.

Nothing happened all day Sunday. Willie slept. Sebastian was up and around by noon, too edgy to sleep, watching the street. By late afternoon it started to rain again, but it was definitely not so cold. And the rain seemed to provide a measure of security—there was less traffic on the street.

It was almost ten o'clock when Margot showed up, coming in through the back as before. Kubeksten had not yet arrived. The boys were staying in the inner room. It was too risky to allow them to move around. Margot began to pace quietly in the front room, looking out of the cracked windows repeatedly.

"There are K.G.B. everywhere," she said once, to no one in particular. "He could have been stopped."

Sebastian realized her concern. Obenoff could not hold out against Chekhov forever. Time was against them, and if Kubeksten should get caught . . . ?

But at eleven o'clock a truck swung ponderously down the driveway that led into the loading dock. Willie was already there and opened the old, battered swinging doors to let him in.

"They are everywhere!" Kubeksten commented fearfully as he stepped down from the cab that had BERLIN STATE CIRCUS painted on the side. "The K.G.B.—the Vopos—I think maybe one car follows me into Clara-Zetkin-Strasse—"

"Did he follow you up this street?" Margot asked him sharply.

Kubeksten wiped his forehead with a large blue handkerchief, then removed his fedora to wipe his hair as well. Willie's flashlight played across his sweaty face. "I cannot say for certain, *Fräulein*," he replied, his voice shaky now as he leaned against the fender. As if he knew, Willie flicked off the light, and they were plunged into the darkness of the loading dock and the fear Kubeksten had brought with him. "I think maybe we should try it tonight—with the balloons, yes?"

They thought about it in silence, because each had prepared himself for another day before tackling the flight. "What about the weather?" Willie asked.

"The wind, it is good," Kubeksten heaved one of those shaky sighs that said it was hardly that good. "It could be warmer—but it is fifty-three degrees. That is enough, I think. I do not think it is safe here now."

"He is right," Margot chimed in conclusively. "As soon as we are ready, we should try it, when the traffic is not heavy outside. Send one of the boys upstairs to watch for any cars," she ordered, and they heard someone scamper up the stairs in the dark. Sebastian was sure it was Dettmann.

"We can use that old elevator shaft," Willie threw in as they risked the light to unhook the aluminum feeder line lashed to the back of the truck.

"Yah," Kubeksten agreed, as if he had already planned it that way.

It took them an hour or more to run the gas feeder line up to the roof, coupling six-foot sections at a time and hooking the line to the shaft with a staple gun. The gun gave off a loud crack, and after each shot they listened, sweating out the possibility of being heard.

It was nearly 12:30 when Dettmann showed up. "Two cars just went by, very slow. They look at the sign on the building, then they go on."

"They'll be back," Margot warned. "They're checking the ruins in the area now, and they probably know Udal has used one of these places for rendezvous before."

"Let's get everybody up here then," Sebastian ordered, and after a few minutes they were all in the small room that smelled of mold and wet plaster. Margot said they should wait until one o'clock, just to be sure. So they waited, hearing each other breathe, their hearts pumping as thousands had done before in this city, waiting for the tramp of boots, for discovery—and death. The contemplation of what lay ahead left Sebastian with a familiar metallic taste, a sign that his tension was burning his body circuits again.

"We have five minutes to come to our senses about this," Willie said then.

"It is too late for that now," Kubeksten responded, his voice cracking a little.

"Then we should say something like 'We who are about to die salute you,'" Willie added wryly.

"That is no talk for children," Kubeksten snapped, sniffing loudly. "Besides, it is not your night to die, Herr Gurnt—you just hold the ropes, yes?"

"So I send you finally—what is the difference?" Willie argued.

"Sentiment is hardly becoming you," Margot cut in, her voice as pinched as the others there in the dark. "By the way, who is going to go first? We'd better be sure now before we get out on the roof."

They tossed it around a few minutes, debating whether to start with one of the children, since whoever took off first, before the Grepos on the wall suspected anything, had the best chance. "No, someone else should try it," Kubeksten argued. "If he does not get high enough over the wall, he is the first to get shot, yes?"

Margot finally insisted Sebastian go. "We're forgetting you have the information that should get to Western Intelligence," she said.

Sebastian might have argued the point, but since risks were involved either way, he let it go. Finally, after a pause during which no one seemed ready to force the move, Kubeksten said, "Maybe the pastor would say something for us now, yes?"

Kubeksten's request caught him off balance, and he suddenly became aware of the fact that he really didn't know them. He didn't want to just say a prayer here—he wanted some light in the room; he wanted to look at them, to touch them, to know them as people. What did they know of God or Christ? The boys—they ate German sausage between black bread; Kubeksten had bad sinuses and a box of cutting tools that probably were too old for the diamond business today. And what of Margot and Willie? He wanted to tell them a lot of things; that even with God in this, they could die tonight, that merely putting the sign of the cross over what was coming didn't guarantee that the wind would be fair or that the Grepos wouldn't shoot; he wanted to tell them that God wasn't giving them these terrible odds in payment for their freedom. He wanted them to understand that, for he didn't want them to go smashing to their death tonight cursing God.

But there wasn't time, and he felt them shift restlessly in the dark as they waited like impatient mourners at a graveside. "God," he said, clearing his throat in a sound that was like a shovel scraping ice, "life and death are in Your hands. But we dare to believe You for life tonight, not because our cause is so honorable or we are so brave . . . but because we believe You are concerned for the weak things that have no power of their own to lay hold on life. . . . We are afraid of this thing, of the balloons, but we take courage in You, who knows the winds and the sky and all that goes into our success or failure tonight. . . . We remember what David said in the Psalm: 'By thee I have run through a troop; and by my God have I leaped over a wall.' We claim this for ourselves too—and thank You for it, in the name of Your Son, Jesus. Amen."

Kubeksten cleared his throat and heaved one of his shaky sighs, and Margot said crisply, "It is time now . . . we must hurry before they come back."

* 12 *
Jump for Your Life

The wind was as light as the touch of a feather on their cheeks. Damp with the earlier rain but not too cold, it was coming out of the southeast as near as Sebastian could tell—so it was blowing right, anyway. They spread the first large balloon out across the roof, working by the fuzzy light of the single lamppost across the empty lot, not daring to try the flashlight up here. Kubeksten ran the hydrogen line to the open neck and turned the nozzle with a wrench. The gas hissed out, slowly expanding the orange-and-blue canvas fabric. The balloon swelled slowly like some beast coming awake, and Kubeksten jumped from one side to the other to make sure it was in the right position. Sebastian tried to think over all the instructions for launch . . . rip valve, descent valve, ballast . . . it was all stuck together like sludge in his brain, and he wondered how much of it the boys would remember in the terror of being driven aloft on a dark night.

Nobody said anything except Kubeksten, who kept talking to the balloon as if it were being born out of pain; everyone simply stood around, watching it reverently as it began to rise slowly to its full capacity—reaching for the sky, straining to connect with its destiny. Inside of twenty minutes, it was almost fully inflated, held down to the roof by the single trail rope Kubeksten had lashed to the sturdy chimney. Ten minutes later he shut off the gas and pulled the nozzle out of the neck of the balloon. Then they hooked the basket on and backed up for a look at the swaying bulk of gaily colored fabric that showed few signs of aeronautical grace.

"If a car comes down that street now, anybody will see this thing without too much trouble," Willie warned in his usual petulant tone.

"Yah," Kubeksten acknowledged quickly. As he removed his fedora to look up at his handiwork, he presented a comical sight with his prim suit and nozzle wrench, as if he had just changed a flat on his way to a dinner party. "But it is good! She wants to rise, yes? That is a good sign!"

"She looks as if she wants to let go with a good belch," Willie responded again acidly, and one of the boys began to smirk nervously over by the chimney.

"You should get ready now, Pastor," Kubeksten said, ignoring Willie's comment. "Remember now . . . when you get in the basket, you pull the string that opens the throat of the balloon to let the gas expand inside, yes? Use ballast carefully . . . not too much . . . only to get high enough over the wall. When you cross the wall, look for the Tiergarten—"

Suddenly there was a warning shout from Margot. The trail rope had snapped loose from the chimney in a shower of frayed strands. Quickly Willie reached up and grabbed the basket as it rose in front of him, obviously hoping he could pull the balloon back down by his weight.

"Let go!" Kubeksten yelled, trying to get hold of Willie's dangling legs as the balloon now jumped skyward under a sudden gust of wind. "Grab the rope!" he shouted at the rest of them, and Sebastian made a dive for it, but it was too late. Willie was now at least thirty feet above them, kicking frantically as he tried to find purchase. Then, just when it looked as if the balloon would take off, it suddenly dipped down, heading in a steep glide for the empty lot below. At that point, Willie was able to pull himself into the basket.

"Throw ballast!" Kubeksten yelled, cupping his hands, and Margot snapped, "You'd better keep it down, or they'll hear you all the way to the wall!"

But the balloon went on down in its collision course before Willie could take any action. The basket hit the ground with a blow that sounded like a paper bag being crushed in the night, and all they could see was Willie grabbing for the ropes above him, pulling himself up to avoid being smashed. Then, as if given a slap on the rump to remind it of its loftier purpose, the balloon began to climb again, staggering on the crosscurrent of wind. Willie was just barely visible in the shroud lines.

The erratic launch had left them all stunned. The boys were bunched up in a tight knot by the chimney in defensive formation against what had occurred, knowing now what to expect. Their confidence had vanished; the balloon had become a joker, promising nothing but a messy kind of way to die. It had snatched from among them the one man who hadn't wanted anything to do with it in the first place.

Kubeksten shook his head, unable to speak for a long time. "It is the wind," he said loudly, as if he were accusing it. "It blows too hard . . . too dangerous to try now!"

Margot came over from her position a few feet away. "You've got to go on with it," she insisted, and Sebastian thought her face showed up too white in the dark.

"*Fräulein*," Kubeksten appealed, "the wind could blow these children clear across Europe to the English Channel—or worse, it could—"

But his argument had hardly gotten under way when they heard the rapid sound of gunfire. Looking to the wall as one, they could make out the single searchlight piercing the sky like a surgeon's knife. Again gunfire thumped into the brittle rib cage of the night, slashing the hopes they had kept alive.

"Herr Gurnt," Kubeksten said for all of them, his voice carrying a wounded tone of finality and defeat.

"He may have made it," Sebastian ventured, fighting off the rising sadness inside him. It should never have come to Willie like that . . . he who had so carefully avoided this kind of involvement.

"And now they know, yes?" Kubeksten added as if completing Sebastian's thoughts. "The Grepos on the wall." And his eyes showed bigger in the half-light. "Now they will be watching—"

"Maybe not," Margot threw in again. "They may think it is only one fool who made the mistake."

"We should send the children now, before they are sure," Sebastian suggested.

"It is you who must go!" she jabbed back at him in a hard tone of impatience.

"If you think I'm going to jump out of here leaving five kids behind to fend for themselves, then you have underestimated me," Sebastian retaliated firmly, trying to pull in the reins of this runaway horse of panic that seemed to jerk at all of them now. "Whatever that thing is with Shattner, I will leave it with God right now. Life takes the priority, right? So let us get on with it; the wind has shifted, Kubeksten, so if they are looking in the same place, maybe we can outfox them yet!"

Kubeksten wiped his sniffling nose with the back of his hand. "Yah," he said, reluctantly and dismally, "but we must hurry . . . the night, it begins to fall in on us, yes?"

So they rolled out the smaller balloons and Kubeksten ran the pipe out again. Sebastian suggested they try sending Fritz and Rolf, the two lightest boys, in hope of saving time. He then took them aside, crouching down to get even with their faces and placing one hand on each of their thin shoulders.

"Is Herr Gurnt dead?" Fritz asked pointedly against the soft hissing sound of the gas behind him.

"Herr Gurnt does not die easily," Sebastian tried. "As he never gave up in the hopscotch, yes?"

172

"Must we die?" Rolf said, putting the question almost as if it were a foregone conclusion.

"No. You don't even have to go if you don't want to. You can stay here. Someone will find a place for you."

"Ulbricht," Fritz said flatly. Then, lifting his eyes to Sebastian again, he said, "If Herr Gurnt is there . . . maybe . . . then I will go . . ."

Rolf thought a moment about it too, biting his lip and looking over his shoulder at the smaller balloon slowly inflating. "I will try it," he said then.

"All right, then, do not be afraid of the balloon," Sebastian returned, trying to get their confidence up. "God goes with you. . . . Just remember the ballast and the descent valve . . . you understand about what to do?"

"You will come, too, in the balloon?" Fritz asked then, shaking aside the other reminders.

"It is my only way out, too," Sebastian replied.

"It will be like Joshua with the horns?"

Sebastian saw the earnestness in those eyes, the desperate desire to believe, to seize hold of a promise beyond what the flimsy balloon offered. Sebastian hesitated; it was one thing to talk about hope in the warm and safe atmosphere of Sunday school back home, quite another here in a night gone ugly. "Like Joshua," Sebastian said, trying to put a smile into it. And he held them close, feeling their fluttering hearts against his own, and he was agonizingly aware of their smallness in his arms against the backdrop of the looming darkness.

Kubeksten said it was time then. They turned to the balloon, which looked even less promising than the larger one. It was half the size and hung above them about fifteen feet off the roof, looking as if it might collapse any minute. But Fritz and Rolf did not hesitate now. They climbed into the basket and wedged themselves into its small space, their hands hanging onto the ropes. Kubeksten, Margot and Dettmann let the trail rope go, but the balloon would not rise. Kubeksten began to flutter around it nervously, trying to coax it into the air with conversation and murmuring his own kind of abracadabra. Finally Sebastian suggested that the boys throw off some of the ballast. Kubeksten consented, although he was afraid they'd throw too much out.

Fritz unloaded the two small sandbags from the ropes. The balloon stayed where it was for just a few seconds, then a sudden gust of wind seemed to catch it, and it rose a few feet, hanging there as if on a string. Then an air pocket grabbed it viciously and the balloon shot upward, careening dangerously, giving the basket a jerk. "Hold on!" Kubeksten shouted, and the two boys grabbed the net ropes, barely keeping themselves from being pitched out. After just one more threatening dip, the balloon rose rapidly and was engulfed in the oblivion of the sky, leaving only the image of the two white faces fixed in their stare downward as earth vanished from them. "They go up too quick!" Kubeksten commented mournfully, but there wasn't time to linger on that thought, and he was already fumbling with the other balloon that would take up the heaviest boy, Paul. From the wall came the sound of motors running and rumbling, stitching new possibilities of crisis into the crazy quilt of events. And there were more lights, too, three long poles of heavy beams exploring the sky where Willie had gone down. They all knew that if the Grepos saw the boys' balloon go over, the whole area was going to get very crowded.

As the balloon inflated, Sebastian got hold of Paul, the quietest of the five—except for Dettmann—but the boy had already been given an injection of euphoria from the apparent ease with which his two companions rose up. He knew he was going it alone, and that it was more difficult that way, but his quiet blue eyes did not waver when he said, "I am not afraid."

"I'll see you over there, Paul," Sebastian said to him simply.

His ascent was more chaotic than that of the others. With the wind slamming across the roof in a new fit of fury, the balloon took off across the empty lot, heading in a beeline for the wall where Willie had disappeared. Then it shot upward and was gone.

Again more lights stabbed the night as if word were being passed down the twenty-six miles of wall that something indeed was in the wind. Kubeksten, who had now begun to puff and pant in his efforts to hurry the launchings, suggested that the other boy ride it out in one of the big balloons with himself and that maybe Dettmann could try it with Sebastian.

They didn't argue the point. There were too many car lights down by the wall now, too much sound of traffic out toward Unter den Linden. So they took the time to run the gas line into one of the bigger balloons. Those next thirty minutes were the longest Sebastian ever spent, fighting the wind that threatened to tear the balloon fabric out of their hands, fighting the fear of discovery, which he was sure had to come any minute.

"It is madness!" Kubeksten shouted once, as they had to battle the balloon down to the roof in the wind. But they went on working, Kubeksten trying to keep the hydrogen flowing into a jumping gas bag as elusive as an animal that refuses to be roped and tied. Sebastian knew then, even as the balloon finally reached its full capacity and bounced dangerously above them, that they wouldn't be able to get another big balloon ready in time. He sensed it was getting colder too, though the wind stayed south. So as he hung onto the net ropes, he told Kubeksten to get into the basket.

"No!" Margot protested from her position directly in front of him, staggering as the balloon tore at her rope. "This is your last chance—"

"Then Kubeksten gets it!" Sebastian shouted back above the wind. Though the old man saw his chances of freedom diminishing along with the rest, he wasn't going to insist. "We'll find our own way out!"

"There isn't any other way!" Margot shrilled back at him. "Will you stop playing the God game here and get into the balloon!"

"Kubeksten!" Sebastian shouted again. "Get into the basket—take Hans with you!" Sebastian would have liked Dettmann to go, but he realized that if any of the boys could fend for himself, it was Dettmann. Kubeksten looked from Sebastian to the girl, who by now had all she could do to hang on to her anchor rope; then he felt Sebastian's foot give him an unceremonious shove in the rump.

Seeing there was no point in debating the matter any further, he picked up his box of cutting tools at the base of the chimney and climbed into the basket. Hans followed.

Margot refused to let go of her rope; her lean body strained with it, and her face was twisted in the slashing lines of the fury she felt now for what Sebastian had done. "You're a crazy, blind, selfish fool!" she screamed at him again. "You'd rather destroy thousands of people and save one or two—do you think I'd go through all this and still not get you over the wall with the information you have?"

"You'll find a way, Margot!" he yelled back, and he smiled at her, trying to defuse her anger. "I have confidence in your ingenuity!"

The wind rose again. Kubeksten, much more professional at this, dropped a sack of ballast, and the balloon jumped off the roof. Margot was sent sprawling flat on her stomach, the rope jerked out of her hands. There was the same chaotic bouncing of the balloon in the wind overhead, but Kubeksten expertly maneuvered against it by using the net ropes. Then this balloon, too, was gone, but moving more northwesterly, toward Bernauer Strasse. Kubeksten was going to be lucky to get out of East Germany at all.

"They come now!" Dettmann called the warning then, even as Sebastian reached down to help Margot up. She shoved his hands away, trying to wipe the water and mud off her leather coat. Sebastian looked down the street at the half-dozen car lights turning in, some flashing the blue of the Vopo wagons.

"Margot, there isn't much time for you to use your

genius," he urged, and he was sure she could see the cars coming too, but she acted as if she didn't much care.

"Go to hell," she said abruptly, speaking in English as though she wanted to make certain he would grasp it. "I put my neck in the noose far enough for you—if you want a way out, then find it yourself!"

"You want to get caught up here with all this evidence around?" he reminded her, trying to jar her loose from her obstinancy. "Besides, you know you haven't gone far enough, Margot. You won't sleep nights until you do everything to get me over—even I know that!"

She looked down to see the blue lights coming up fast. For a few seconds she didn't move, and Sebastian was almost sure she was going to let them find them here. But then, as if struck by the ultimate dimension of it all, she said in a snapping tone: "Downstairs!"

Sebastian had no idea what she had in mind, but she was too smart not to have laid out the back-up possibilities in case the balloons failed. They headed down the stairs toward the loading dock as the sound of car tires slashed to a stop in front of the building. As they moved over the bomb in the stairway, she stopped. "You have Willie's flashlight?" she asked. Sebastian pulled it out of his coat pocket. "Shine it on the bomb there. . . . You have Kubeksten's nozzle wrench?" Sebastian handed it to her as he put on the light. He watched her with a sense of recoil building within him and at the same time some wonder at her coolness as she put the thin handle of the wrench through the large loop of the cotter pin.

"That's a messy way to end it," he commented, licking an itchy drop of sweat off his upper lip.

"It's all the genius I've got left," she poked back at him, yanking the cotter pin loose and moving down the stairs in quick leaps as the sound of the ticking came out loudly from the suddenly awakened heart of the bomb.

She took Sebastian and Dettmann down a rickety ladder under the loading dock into a smaller room that must have been a heating plant at one time. At any minute

Sebastian expected the bomb to go off—all he would remember would be a split second of flame and brick—and he had the crazy desire to stop right there for those few seconds and introduce himself to her properly—and to Dettmann. But she did not seem to be giving it the same regard as he, as she swung the beam of the flashlight around the floor until it caught the handle of a drain cover. "That's it," she said tightly, as if she had discovered the safe. "Pull that cover up . . ." He reached down to yank at the two rusty handles, but the cover was stuck with muck and he couldn't budge it. Dettmann laid his small, pudgy hands over his, and after much straining, it came, giving very slowly until finally Margot was able to squeeze her hands underneath and push. Sebastian stared into the yard-wide hole with the water rushing by below, looking black and turbid. "So it's into the sewers, is it?"

"Hurry," she said sharply to him, and Sebastian heard the voices upstairs now, then a shout of warning, followed by the hasty rattle of retreat outside and the sound of cars jumping away. Sebastian helped Dettmann into the hole and onto the rusty ladder that hung loosely in place. Then Margot went down, he following. The sewer was running high, probably because of heavy rains, and as Sebastian pushed by Dettmann on the ladder, he noticed that the boy didn't want to let go, but stayed at the bottom, the water rushing over his belt, his hands hanging on tight to the lower rung. Margot had already jumped into the water, keeping herself from being swept along by hanging onto the protruding bricks on the opposite wall of the narrow cavern.

Sebastian got in and turned to reach up for Dettmann. "You can hang on to me, Christian," he said, his voice echoing hollowly in the dim tunnel. Suddenly he realized that Dettmann couldn't swim, and the first cloud of fear he had ever seen passed across the boy's stoic face.

Sebastian threw aside his topcoat. "You can climb on my back and put your arms around my neck."

The boy hesitated, but finally reached out and jumped

off. Sebastian hoisted him to a more comfortable position, feeling that there wasn't any weight to the boy at all—nothing more than skin and bones. Then Sebastian moved out into the cold, slimy water, ignoring the nauseating smells, intent only on negotiating the slippery tunnel floor and the water that came up to his chest. Margot struggled on her own a few feet behind, coughing on the acrid odor of lime that ran with the sewage. The only light was from small light bulbs that glowed every fifty feet or so, hung behind dirty wire mesh. Sometimes when they were in complete darkness, caught in the swirling eddies, Dettmann's arms would tighten around Sebastian's neck and his legs dig in deeper. The rushing water seemed caught in a much too narrow passage, and Sebastian couldn't help wondering if it wasn't getting higher.

Finally, after what seemed a long time of slipping and sliding in the muck, the three of them paused under a dim light, trying to get their breath.

"You have a pretty fast flush in the water system," he commented to Margot.

They were clinging to the same metal spar that protruded from the wall. She was trembling in the cold, the end of her long hair soaked with slime, her leather waistcoat greasy. She didn't answer right away, seemingly too exhausted. "When it rains as it has lately, they open the gates to the Spree," she finally replied, not bothering to look at him, busying herself with wiping the dirty water off her face. "So it runs fast . . ."

Sebastian was conscious again of Dettmann's small, hard knuckles pressing into his Adam's apple, squeezing harder as the water got rougher.

"How about the bomb," he asked then, "and our pursuers?"

"That bomb probably won't go off," she replied. "Only one in twenty ever does—too old. But they don't know that. The ticking will keep them out of the building, anyway . . ."

"You had it all figured, didn't you?"

She flicked a hard glance at him. "I never intended a trip like this," she said brusquely. "And I didn't plan on gambling with a bomb."

"I think your values are improving," he replied, snorting against the lime fumes.

"The value of my own life is—very much so," she retorted. "I didn't stand much chance with the Vopos either . . . so don't get the idea I'm cutting corners just for you."

"Never," he quipped, and he tried a smile on her that didn't get him anywhere. "So how far do we go in this then?" he asked, feeling the cold and the bone-weary exhaustion.

"I don't know exactly," she said, turning to look ahead into the murky glow of the tunnel. "When we come to the branch-off, not too far, I'll know then."

He didn't talk any more, as he wanted to get on with it. He moved out into the swirling, liquid garbage, pulling Dettmann up tighter on his back. It was no way to die— this. He would rather smash into the ground with a balloon. But to drown, swallowing a city's waste, to be vomited out into the Spree like some indigestible flotsam that even the sewer couldn't take . . . and he knew this wasn't a remote possibility. They could close the gates to the Spree any time, and the backup would finish them off in seconds. He read it in Margot's eyes, just for an instant, when she looked uncertainly ahead.

And he wanted to hurry, to push against the rush of water, to find firmer footing in this tunnel sticky with silt. It seemed a long, long time since he'd crossed Checkpoint Charlie on that bus for the Jubilee. And he sensed the flame dying in him, as if someone had put a glass over it and cut off the oxygen. And for one awful moment he allowed himself to ask if it was really necessary; was it so important to run this crooked mile of Johnny's? He hadn't much to show for it—he had lost Willie probably, and who knew where the boys were now or even Kubeksten? What had he left behind here, anyway? He had run in another man's shoes, copied another man's corruption . . . there hadn't even been time to project his own image after he was found out. So maybe he was pushing too far . . . maybe there were boundaries after all that even a man of God shouldn't cross. Maybe the boy he carried on his back didn't need any of this either, stumbling around in this smelly place, prowling in the stinking intestines of a city, fighting the ugly death that swirled around him. Was it so bad in East Berlin, anyway? Maybe Willie was right—there were no tracks of God here and maybe there shouldn't be any.

And then he stopped, because suddenly he felt he ought to tell Margot it was all wrong, that he was asking too much of her, of Dettmann, of all of them.

But as he stopped, half-staggering with the rush of water, he saw the tunnel branch off into two tributaries. He felt Margot bump him from behind as she tried to stand up against the current that had gotten stronger here. She moved around him for a grip on the greasy wall a few feet away, coughing and gagging on the lime gas. He stood there, half-sliding in the mud, peering at the steel fence that blocked their way to the right; it was like a picket fence, the flat shafts running from the roof of the cavern down under the water to the floor. He remembered Johnny's talking about this as "Ulbricht's answer to sewer rats who try to make it out."

He looked to the left then, to where the tunnel narrowed to a smaller culvertlike pipe. The water rushed into it with a foaming, thrashing sound; there was maybe a foot open at the top. He shifted Dettmann's weight on his back again, trying to compute their chances.

"Where does that lead?" he said to Margot, his voice booming off the tunnel walls.

"Right under the Office of Internal Affairs on Leipziger Strasse," she replied factually, her voice sounding a bit shrill now. He half turned to look at her, but her glance did not waver. Her blue lips and her plastered hair left her with an exposed, almost vulnerable, look, and he knew then that she wasn't sure of their chances either.

"So what happens when we get there?" he shouted to her.

"You have your best chance for the wall there," she said pointedly.

He understood now why no steel fence covered that small avenue of excape; Ulbricht's engineers figured anybody trying to go through would land in the flypaper anyway.

"Is it big enough?" he shouted at her again.

"High enough for you to stand in it," she remarked.

"How long?"

"About fifty yards . . ."

Fifty yards didn't seem too long. But with only a foot or so of air at the top, in pitch darkness, with water tugging at his legs, Dettmann on his back, it would be more like fifty miles. He felt the boy stir as if he had made his own calculations and wanted to back off.

"Now Christian, just remember," Sebastian said, trying to be light about it, moving slowly to the mouth of the pipe, "hang on to me with all you got . . . don't jump off, yes? We are going to be the first tunnel rats to do what Ulbricht never expected, yes?" And he felt the squeeze of the boy's arms and legs like a vise. "Now we have lots of room at the top to breathe . . . we'll just let the water take us along . . . you ready now, Christian?"

The boy said nothing. There was nothing really to say. Ready or not, this was the way the whole thing had shaped up. Sebastian turned once before stepping into the pipe and looked back at Margot; she was still holding onto the greasy walls of the tunnel, probably debating whether she had to risk this at all. She might make it back the way she had come—at least she had a better chance there than he. But it was a long way, and he called to her above the sound of the water, "They may close the gates to the Spree at any time . . . you could get caught back there, you know that?"

He knew that she knew it the moment she decided to

commit them to the sewer. But for a few brief seconds she was willing to reconsider, for the ride in that pipe offered little more.

"Take off that strait jacket you're wearing," he told her. "There isn't room enough in that pipe!" She took it off while he tried to hold her against the rush of the current, which was getting stronger by the minute now. Her white turtle-neck sweater turned a dirty gray in the swirling water. Their eyes locked for just a second before he turned to the pipe; it was a kind of salute, he thought. They were for this brief second or two as one—ideology, world view, none of this mattered now. "Don't forget to hold your nose!" he tried banter with her. He gave her a quick smile and thought he saw that girlish look in her eyes again, perhaps as a token of acknowledgment.

Then he entered the pipe. And he hadn't been in it ten seconds before he knew it was a terrible mistake, beyond what he had even remotely imagined. The water thundered to confirm it while Dettmann gave off a low moan of terror in his left ear.

* 13 *
Which Way to Die?

Major General Bill Kelland sipped at his sixth cup of coffee in an hour. The plot room of the AACN was blue with smoke and stuffy with the smell of men who had struggled too long over a problem. Above it hovered that other smell—the pungent odor of mounting tension. It was as if someone were tightening the strings on an instrument that was called East-West Relations; and Kelland felt that one more turn, and something had to blow up.

Three of them were there now—Colonel Bollweg, Colonel Jacques Monteau of France, Major Robert Heath of Britain. They had been at it now around the clock since Wednesday, when the counterintelligence in East Berlin reported the shooting. They finally had the name of the man on the run: Kurt Udal. They had his profile on teletyped sheets in front of them—everything from his tattoos to the corns on his feet and his dual espionage history.

But while they were trying to piece it together, Kelland was watching other code releases showing that the Russian troop movements had begun on the other side. It was beginning to bother him. It was now three o'clock on Monday morning, and the Russian battalions were not thinking about Tuesday's celebrations but were reported moving to strategic positions by the wall. The man who had tried it in the circus balloon had pulled the stopper on everything. Willie Gurnt—his name had come through on the profile sheets with Udal's. He had just made it at that, falling twenty feet inside the western zone at the Brandenburg Gate, but shot up very badly. And Kelland pondered it again, especially the strange last words the man said before he passed out, "Thy servant Jacob is behind us . . ."

So they had tried to figure out what it meant, even to having Major Heath read the entire Jacob and Esau story for a clue. But it was Colonel Max Bollweg who brought the first light. "We just received an official call from Emil Shattner of the Gehlen Bureau . . ." Kelland looked up quickly, as did Monteau and Heath, for their earlier attempts to get something out of Shattner had proved fruitless. "He says," Bollweg went on in his crisp German accent, "that Udal is coming over carrying contraband: secret documents to be passed on to clandestine interests not sympathetic to East or West. They go under the code name 'The Five Books of Moses.' Shattner says at all costs, if Udal makes it over, he is to be apprehended, or shot on sight if he resists. If he lives, he belongs to the Gehlen Bureau for interrogation."

Heath grunted, for it was strange for Shattner to put such a price on a double agent that no one really knew much about in the network. But it was clear now to Kelland what he had to do.

"Alert all units," he said to Bollweg. "Stand-by troop orders to move in five hours. Get General Thorpe of NATO in Brussels on the line, too. Then try to get Chekhov and find out why he is holding those American clergymen over there at the Jubilee. Tell Shattner he can have his man Udal if we get him, but we must know the nature of the contraband first. And no travel permits issued and no news releases . . . got it?"

Bollweg nodded and left. There was a heavy silence in the room except for the faint sound of the teletypes in an outer room.

"Too bad we can't do anything for the poor bugger," Heath finally said, taking off his glasses, rubbing his tired, bloodshot eyes. Heath looked and acted like an English butler.

"Who?"

"Udal. It seems it would be to our advantage if we could nail down the man who seems to be stirring up the trouble on both sides."

"He really doesn't belong to anybody," Kelland said with a sigh, wondering how long he could hold the lid on what was building up outside in Berlin now. "Our people don't know him. Shattner is the only one who seems to have a line on him, so it would be his move now. It seems Udal has something important enough for both sides to want him pretty badly—our job now is to make sure they don't slam into each other dropping on the fellow."

"Well," Monteau said with a sigh, shoving his spectacles high up on his forehead and lifting his eyes off the open Bible in front of him to Kelland, "this man Gurnt must know the Genesis account very well to just yank a verse out like that. Is Jacob Udal, then? And if Udal is carrying contraband, why does Gurnt want to tip it off?"

"More than that, why does he send this man Gurnt out first?" Kelland added. "I should think he'd try for it before the Grepos got wise."

"Maybe Gurnt's a decoy," Heath suggested.

"Maybe," Kelland admitted, staring down at the profile sheets in front of him again. "Or maybe he's part of the smuggling job, and when he got iced over the wall, he figured the best thing he could do for Udal was try to let us know he's coming and help him. The Bible verse is undoubtedly part of the operation cover."

"Well, we know Udal over there is running out of percentages," Heath said with a yawn. "If he tries anything as crazy as the balloons, the Grepos will have him . . . and I'm sure Chekhov has plugged the other holes up by now."

"One thing is sure," Kelland said. He got up and

walked slowly around the room, his hands held behind his back, his eyes on the floor. "We've got to get him, because as long as he's running free, the temperature is bound to go up on both sides of the wall. Alive or dead, gentlemen, we've got to get him, and within the next few hours. Let's hope he's got something up his sleeve that'll get him over—otherwise, this could be a very long war."

It was dark and wet in that small pipe. Sebastian knew by the feel of the water rushing around him that he could get knocked off his feet any minute. Though he managed to breathe by keeping his head close to the ceiling, now and then he felt the water come up over his ears and into his mouth and Dettmann would moan again. He called to Margot in the dark, and after a long pause got the answer, a kind of gagging assurance that she was still there behind him—somewhere.

"Don't be afraid, Christian," he said, his voice sounding tinny in the metal culvert. "We don't have far to go."

But it was a long way. And each step seemed to be the prelude to disaster. It was impossible to maintain bearings without light, and it was like floating in limbo. And Sebastian wondered if, when they got to the end, they might run into one of those fence traps—just one more guarantee by Ulbricht's engineers that no one who dared this kind of journey could expect to get through. In that case they would die there, pinned up against the fence.

He didn't know how far he had gone, his head bumping the ceiling, when he became conscious that the air space on top was getting smaller. He found himself pushing himself upward, with Dettmann squirming to do the same.

"The water is rising," Margot called from behind him. "Go faster! They are starting to close the gates!"

Sebastian kept looking for a sign of light ahead, something that would indicate the end of this hell—but he couldn't see anything yet. He felt the water begin to grab him harder around the legs as it picked up speed, and tried to use the sides of the pipe to keep from being swept headlong down the drain. If that happened, he would not be able to hold on to Dettmann. He told himself he was not afraid to die here . . . but he wanted Dettmann to have a chance.

And then he saw just a fingernail of light ahead, coming up through the rushing water, beckoning at the same time as he felt his legs go out from under him and heard Dettmann cry out. Sebastian steadied himself against the wall and swung Dettmann off his back and in front of him where he could hold him with both arms. And then the water rushed over them, and he let himself go. Twice he came up to the ceiling for air, dragging Dettmann with him, shoving the boy up as he did so, giving him a second to breathe. Then they were under again.

How long that plunge lasted, he couldn't tell, but when his lungs refused to take it any more, he felt himself shoved upward—coasting on air, it seemed—and the next minute he knew he had passed from the rushing pull of the pipe through a sudden drop into another kind of water, much quieter.

He shot to the surface, opened his eyes and looked around. He was surprised to see he still had Dettmann in one arm; the boy was shaking his head, coughing and gagging. Sebastian saw that they were in a side eddy; ahead of them was a cement dock, and there were bright lights in the ceiling. The water rushed on by them on its way to the outlet into the Spree. Sebastian pushed wearily to the dock and shoved Dettmann up onto it, then turned to look for Margot. He couldn't see her at first. He had moved out in the main eddy toward the pipe when she bobbed up like a cork a few feet away. He grabbed her by the shoulders and helped her onto the dock. They all lay quietly for a while, none of them wanting to move, too exhausted, too cold, almost hugging the cement that was such a welcome relief from the slippery slime of the sewer. Sebastian took time to look around. They were on an island of cement, the sewer water completely surrounding them. About ten feet ahead of them was a small concrete cubicle which had to be some kind of sentry post placed here to pick off anybody who would try that pipe. It was empty now, perhaps because nobody in the building expected anyone to be crazy enough to try the pipe with the Spree gates closed.

Margot had gotten up slowly then. She was soaked through and still trembling from the cold. "We must go," she said without looking back at either Sebastian or Dettmann, her voice almost lost in the sound of the water. They got up to follow her to the cubicle, and Sebastian caught up to her there and said, "What do you have in mind?" his voice cracking from the exhaustion.

She still didn't look at him. She was staring up the long slope of the cement steps instead. "I said the chance for the wall was better here," she replied. "We'd better go on up . . . nobody is on duty in the Ministry now except maybe two security guards."

"Is that all?" Sebastian replied, trying to be jaunty and winking at Dettmann, who dropped his eyes, still embarrassed by this attempt at intimacy.

She didn't say anything; instead, she walked on up the steps, and Sebastian and Dettmann finally followed. Sebastian watched the long line of her back as it moved rhythmically up the stairs ahead of him, wondering what she thought now, what torments she was having, leading two "enemies of the state" through the very territory designed to entrap anyone with even a thought of escape. He couldn't help but sympathize with her—she was being dragged headlong into a plot that could at any moment blow up in her face.

When they got to the fourth-floor landing, she took them through the dark, silent offices, staying close to the walls, pausing now and then to listen, to watch. Finally they came out on the far side of the building, and she pushed a door open to what appeared to be an attached gable with cardboard barrels stacked around the sides. They moved to a window that overlooked a long, sliding roof. Below them, beyond the pitch of the roof, lights showed up the one hundred yards or so of open field. As he looked north, he saw the cement watchtower shaped like an oil tank, partly obscured by the construction pilings stashed around. A crane sat about twenty yards this side of the tower; its long boom stabbed skyward, half concealing it. He took in the tank barricades farther out, the low "x"-shaped steel structures that prevented any vehicle from getting through.

"Sit down by that radiator, Christian," Sebastian said quietly to the boy, who found it hard to control his shivers in the damp room. He needed no prodding. He slid down to the floor and put his back to the little heat that was there. His eyes stayed on them, though, always watchful—but more on Sebastian now, for some reason. "This has to be Potsdamer Platz," Sebastian went on, keeping his voice down to a half whisper. "It's a long way to run out there. . . . You said this was the best place to try it?"

She stepped back out of the light of the window and into the shadows, as if she didn't want to have to be seen while she explained. "It is the best," she said gratingly, impatient with his insistence on descriptions at this late hour. "There are no dogs for one—they are pouring cement for the new kennels. And no trip wires. That old crane there will block their vision for the first thirty yards anyway. It will be more difficult for them to get their sights on you out there at that range."

"You must have studied this thing quite a while," he said to her, half to himself, still looking out of the window across the long field.

"It is my job to work over the security designs of the wall at times." Her voice had an irritable note.

"How about the last ten yards near the wall?" he asked. "The red carpet with the toothpick spikes . . . ?"

"They have torn that up. . . . Construction is building a new wall out there; you can see part of it."

He squinted through the dirty glass until he saw the

low barricade of cement about twenty feet out from the old wall.

"Anything else?" he continued probing, trying to pick up all he had going for him now.

She hesitated a minute. "There are the mines," she said then, her voice gone tight despite her effort to be casual about it.

Sebastian sighed, rubbing at the grease that was turning to a hard crust on his face, hating the smell of the sewage on him. "Just mines; is that all?" he quipped, but it didn't come off very well.

"It is possible they have removed them for the trucks to go in there," she contradicted his sardonic tone. "You can see the dark place in the grass where they have gone in and out . . ."

Sebastian looked, but he could not see anything different in the grass where she pointed. He wanted to go on adding up the possibilities with her, but a sound from inside moved her to lift the window sash quickly, wincing as it scraped against the warped wood. "You'd better get on the roof now," she said quickly.

Sebastian dropped down to where Dettmann sat hugging his knees in front of the radiator. His upturned eyes were almost pleading, and he did not try to move his shoulder from under Sebastian's hand. For that one moment in time Sebastian sensed the response, the first real note of communion between them, the first hint that the boy felt knitted to him by what they had experienced.

"You want to make history, Christian?" Sebastian said softly to him, feeling the wet wool of the sweater under his palm. "You want to beat the wall for all those people who died trying? Shall we give Ulbricht a stomach ache for his breakfast?"

What else was there on which to appeal to a young life who deserved many more years? How else could he put it to the boy, who knew only too well that nobody ever really made it over the wall this way? But for the moment, perhaps, the boy could see beyond the death that awaited them—for there was no way back now either. His chances were as good running for his life out there as facing what he would have to go through with Chekhov.

And there was a slight trace of a smile crossing his small mouth that trembled spasmodically with the cold, maybe just a trace of softening in the eyes, as if perhaps he had seen for a split second the glory of the challenge. And as he reached out to grab Sebastian's arm, using it to pull himself up, there passed between them something peculiarly intimate, the awkward pressure of confidence that whatever happened, it would be all right. And then he stood there by himself, waiting, not accepting any more props from Sebastian, climbing now his own hill of destiny, wanting to walk up that mountain by himself.

The sound came to them again, the sound of boots in the inner corridor, and they went out the window hurriedly—Dettmann first, then Sebastian and then Margot, who had no other choice at the moment. It was chilly on the roof, and there were shadows here from the overhang above them; the arc lights over the open field did not diffuse this far. And as they lay flat there on the slope of the roof, heads down, well away from the window, Sebastian threw one arm across Dettmann in a protective gesture on his left, while he was conscious of Margot on his right, her shoulder touching his, the closest she'd been to him since the kiss—and it was as though all three of them huddled to draw strength and warmth from one another.

They waited as the Grepo guard strolled up the blacktop road about thirty yards away, moving from their left across their vision, heading toward the tower beyond the crane, his rifle slung casually over his shoulder. While they waited, Sebastian sensed something of the conflict building again in Margot.

"There is no path through those mines," he said then, reaching out to help her to what she had to do. "You know where they are because it is fixed in your mind from the charts—"

"I cannot go," she said with finality, knowing what he was after. "I have come far enough."

"How far is enough, Margot?"

"I must stay here," she snapped. "If you must die, then I still have time to get to Chekhov to inform the other side—"

"Have you?" he contradicted. "After we make our try, live or die, Chekhov will know that we tried it here at Leipziger Strasse off Potsdamer Platz. And there is no way for us to do this unless someone got us into the Ministry building and out here on the roof, right? And that narrows it down to you, Margot."

She didn't answer him directly, but kept her eyes on the Grepo moving off the stage to their right. Now and then her body jerked with the spasms of cold.

"So it is my life you demand now too, is it?" she returned with a grating harshness in her voice. "That hungry God of yours demands the full sacrifice; is that it?"

"No, Margot," he said softly, looking once over his shoulder toward the window, sensing the shrinking of the perimeter of time. "If you want forgiveness for what you did to your parents, then ask God for it. You can't win that by running a hundred miles for me or Dettmann . . ."

"There is no time for theology here," she countered with a snap, but he thought he detected a faint catch in her hoarse, urgent whisper.

"All right, but you know it now for the record. . . ."

"There is hardly time for the record."

"And not much time left to die either," he replied. "But there's enough anyway to be sure where you stand—"

"I know where I stand. You have your cause; I have mine."

"But yours won't let you sleep nights, Margot. I'm offering a more workable solution to your real problem. Udal never gave you that; that's why you hated him. Maybe that's why I came all this way, just to give you the remedy. Is that so illogical?"

"It is irrelevant," she said flatly.

"Okay." He saw that the Grepo was gone now, and the sky beyond the lights was beginning to show a slice of paleness, the first finger of dawn gripping the rim of the night. "But if you go back now, you don't prove anything for all your careful planning. You know it as well as I do. You'll still have your conscience. You need a touch of humanity, Margot, beyond those cold records you keep on people over here. So here's your chance—you want to die for something meaningful, giving someone else a chance at life, or do you want the cold, lifeless machine of Chekhov's?"

She didn't answer. Instead, she pressed her face into her hands, and it was the first real sign of the bending power of truth. He wanted badly to reach out and touch her; to soften the sharp, lancing words.

"Come on, Christian," he said. "We've got a date for breakfast on the other side . . . all right?" And he turned to look into the boy's face only a foot from his, and the hard lines that had given him that pugnacious look, the sagging pockets of sadness and bitterness around his mouth and eyes, had almost disappeared. He was suddenly a boy of twelve—something clean and vibrant had come into him.

"I am ready," he said simply, and there was deep meaning in the simple words.

They moved down the slope of the roof, leaving Margot still lying there. They slid down the gutter pipe and landed in the shadows of the Ministry building. Sebastian waited, studying the ground ahead of him, picking his course, but giving her time. After a few minutes Dettmann touched his arm, and he looked up to see her coming down the pipe. He didn't say anything, nor did he look at her, sparing her that much, anyway. After a long pause she said, "You will follow me . . . stay in a single line . . . and don't stop running, whatever happens."

For a moment Sebastian wanted to embrace them both. Instead, he took her hand in his, then Dettmann's in the other—hers trembled some, but she did not remove it; Dettmann's was strangely warm and moist. "God go with us," he said simply, squeezing those hands once, then letting them loose.

She took off her low-heeled shoes and tossed them aside, and with just one look in both directions, started out in a low, crouching run. Dettmann was next as Sebastian ordered, for he wanted the boy to get as much protection as possible from himself. He felt the lights hit them first—those arc lamps with their powerful beams flooding them with exposure, nailing them like so many butterflies against the wallboard of the grass. He noted Margot's legs pumping with the urgency of an athlete; Dettmann ran in jerky motions, his uncoordinated body waving from side to side. . . .

Now they were out twenty yards, even with the crane, and someone was shouting from the direction of that concrete tower. Just then Sebastian saw Dettmann jump completely out of line behind Margot, cut swiftly to the right, and head straight for the crane. Sebastian swung out with him, trying to lay hold of him, feeling the rising pressure in his throat, trying to shout the question and the warning at the same time. But Dettmann was too swift for him, and Margot had swung back now too, grabbing Sebastian, restraining him, even fighting him. "Let him go!" she yelled shrilly at him, and when he continued to fight her, she shoved him so hard that he stumbled backward. "He's doing what he wants to do! You can't help him by trying to stop him; you can only defeat him!"

An automatic weapon opened up then from the tower; he saw the flash of the muzzle, felt the thumping bullets dig ripping holes in the sod. He didn't understand it—about Dettmann. But he knew it was too late to stop him now. He saw him reach the cab, open the door and climb in. It was a purposeful, deliberate move, something the boy must have rehearsed in his mind. So now all he could do was turn and run, following Margot, feeling death raining on them, but somehow not caring—not with Dettmann gone—and yet knowing he had to run for a chance to win, for that was what the boy was trying to give him in the only way he knew. . . .

It was only a matter of a few seconds now before those guns found them. . . . The firing was meanly staccato, the bullets closer in their final search, the air snapping overhead. They reached the "x"-shaped tank-trap structures and climbed over, slowing down to negotiate them—the bullets ricocheted off. They fell to the other side, huddling for a moment under the structures, and Sebastian looked back and saw what was happening then. The crane was coughing smoke from its stack, an animal coming alive, snorting and trumpeting. As he watched, just barely seeing the little head in the cab, the huge arm of the crane began to move to the left, dragging that monstrous steel ball a few feet off the ground, swinging it ponderously back, high—and then it came like a giant pendulum, rushing in a murderous arc, gaining terrible speed with the arm of the crane pulling it . . . and it struck the tower with the sound of matchboxes being smashed under a boot. . . . The dust and brick and cement shot skyward like the spouting of water and blood from a mortally wounded whale. . . . The ball went on through, dripping with the waste of its destruction, then swinging back again. . . .

"Come on!" Margot yelled at him. He pulled himself up numbly from the ground, forcing himself on, wanting to stay there, to watch it all, hoping beyond hope that Dettmann would make it out. The guns on the tower were silent, but Sebastian noticed the armored car coming up from the far end of the field, racing on the blacktop, its turret gun firing at the crane, then out at them. He saw the rest of it only in snatches, over his shoulder as he ran . . . the big ball coming down on its ponderous arc, catching the armored car and clipping the turret gun clean off with one slicing blow, knocking the vehicle over on its side like a toy . . . men jumping out, firing at the crane . . . and more firing coming at him and Margot too, from the right this time, as another armored car came up

196

from that direction, bouncing across the field toward them. . . .

"Where are the mines?" he yelled. She wasn't slowing down, but was running a kind of plumb-line course, so he knew she was threading the needle here. Behind him he heard the terrible sounds of destruction, of guns, explosions, ripping holes into the early dawn—and he dared not look back again, for he knew they were on Dettmann, tearing at him with their steel claws, desperate now to stop those little moist hands that gripped the controls, that pounded havoc into the reputation of this impenetrable wall. And now Margot had reached the last ten-yard strip, that which had been plowed up by the construction machines and freed of spikes, and she ran headlong for the low barrier that was the beginning of the new wall construction. Sebastian caught the faces peering gingerly over the top of the old wall from the observation platform on the western side, and saw the rope someone had dropped down the side for them. But the firing had become a continual sound, roaring like some outraged monster pawing the ground, a lot of it slamming around them as they ran, not missing by much . . . and then they were at the new barrier, diving behind it as the bullets smashed into the cement block. Over it all, Sebastian heard the explosion that rocked hollowly above the snapping fire, and he jumped up to look back. The light tank was on the blacktop now and was firing deliberately into the crane. Already the cab was a shambles, smoke from it curling skyward above the arc lamps . . . and still that tank fired, pouring merciless fire into the wreck, and Sebastian dropped back behind the barrier, not wanting to witness anything more.

"Take the rope!" Margot yelled at him. When he hesitated, she seized it and shoved it into his stomach. "There's an armored car coming up on us fast!"

"You go!" he shouted back.

"Are you going to spoil what that boy did for you?" she rammed back at him. Her face was white, her eyes big with the action, but there was insistence there now that he not betray the death that had given him a way out. He took the rope and started climbing the slippery wall, his feet sliding on the wet surfaces. The faces peered down at him, sometimes ducking for protection. He felt the bullets smash the wall and knock chips of brick into his face; he kept trying to climb—he was halfway up now—but could not find purchase with his feet. Then someone began pulling on the rope, and he went up, finally falling over the barbed wire at the top into willing hands.

He turned quickly, dropping the rope back, looking down as she grabbed it. "Can't somebody stop that armored car?" he shouted to the others in German. But they were only policemen, not really equipped to do a job like that. He looked down at her again and shouted, "Take hold, Margot! I'll pull you up!"

She grabbed the rope more firmly then, deciding to make the try though the armored car was heading straight for her, trying to follow the invisible line of safety through the mine field. He held the rope, feeling three or four hands pulling with him, all of them oblivious of the fire . . . she was almost up, and he reached down to grab her hand, took hold of it in his own, and felt the bullets slam into her there. Her body jumped with it, and her hand went limp for a moment, but he hung on harder. Someone grabbed his belt to keep him from falling over the side. Then the explosion came, blinding him for a second, and a shower of debris came down on him. The armored car had hit the mine field. But he wasn't looking there; he was holding onto that hand, looking down into that upturned face and straining to lift her. There was no agony in that face now. There might have been just a trace of a smile on the pale mouth, the innocent girlish look she had worn listening to *Edelweiss* in that restaurant. His hand was gripping her hand hard, and feeling through that touch the communication of her heart. . . . He thought she was trying to say something to him . . . her lips moved . . . and her eyes carried a quiet resignation, and it was as

198

if she were telling him it was all right.

Then he got her up and over the barrier and down gently on the platform floor as someone kept shouting to give him room. And he held her in his arms while the sirens sounded in the dawn and the police klaxons hooted their nervous wail. A white-coated man from an ambulance put a stethoscope to her chest and listened, then slowly removed it and looked at him with a kind of fright in his brown eyes. "I'm sorry, sir . . ."

Sebastian nodded slowly, wanting to be sure the man understood that it was all right, that it wasn't his fault. But he held her there a long time, feeling nothing but the numbness of the loss in his own body, finding it hard to believe that her strength, her magnificent running form of just a few moments ago were forever stilled. He watched the blood turn her turtle neck to a dirty ink, soaking through the crusted sewage and grime of her long journey in the night. Slowly he brushed her hair back from her face, until it was as it was when he first saw her in the films with Johnny Vandermeer—only now there was no beguilement, no detachment; and he saw the serenity sweeping slowly across her face from somewhere inside her, as if the tight fist that had held her captive for so long had now relaxed; and the tired lines vanished around her mouth and under her eyes to leave her with the pure beauty that was hers. It seemed strangely quiet there; the policemen had taken off their caps in respect. They knew what he felt, for they had lived with this a long time.

He carried her down the steps himself and placed her on the ambulance cot, then slowly pulled the blanket over her face and let them take her away. As the ambulance drove off, a man in a German officer's uniform clicked his heels and said, "Herr Udal, I am ordered to place you under arrest . . . you will follow me, please?"

He nodded dumbly, knowing it had to come to this, but taking a moment to watch the blue light of the ambulance fade up the street until it was gone.

* 14 *
The Last Crooked Mile

They poured a cup of coffee for him as he told them the whole thing from the beginning—from the moment Johnny Vandermeer met him at the Siegessäule, to the Jacob and Esau plan, the balloons, the flight in the sewer and the final attempt at the wall. He knew it did not sound convincing—it had a predominant note of absurdity even—and he was still paralyzed by the shock of losing Margot and Dettmann. But at least he felt some sympathy from Kelland, who stood quietly behind his desk in his neat military uniform, not pushing, taking his time.

It was Shattner, sitting across from him in front of the desk, who kept the heat on him, pinching that half-smoked cigarette from underneath as he held it to his mouth. His eyes were half-hidden behind those glasses, and his hat was perched on his head as usual.

Kelland sighed then as if he would rather not go on with this and said, "I have to hold you, Herr Udal, for violation of the Official Secret Act of NATO. You have knowledge of documents detrimental to NATO Security—if you give us the information we need, the charges might go easier."

"I am not Udal," Sebastian said flatly, fighting off the dizzying spasm of exhaustion that grabbed him unmercifully, knowing he had to keep ahead of Shattner boring in for the kill. "I am Raymond Sebastian, an American clergyman . . ."

So they went through it bit by bit, Shattner countering every defense of Sebastian's. Udal's papers were on him, and they checked the tattooed numbers on his arm that Shattner had put on with the tattoo needles, but which now verified Shattner's claim that only Udal had those numbers on him. "Find those kids in the balloons," Sebastian insisted. "Or there's a man named Langley on the other side who was in the Jubilee—he'll verify the double image—"

"We have no reports on balloon sightings, other than Gurnt's," Kelland returned. "And Colonel Chekhov of the K.G.B. won't release any of the Americans in the Jubilee until we return you—Herr Udal—back to him." Kelland added that they had checked the incoming Pan American flight for any name of Sebastian, and even the German Hilton. There was nothing. Finally Sebastian suggested wiring his former church in Nashville, Wisconsin, for verification. Kelland showed interest in this, but Shattner didn't bother to protest. He knew it would take too much time to make verification in that direction.

At last Sebastian decided to put it on the line. He pulled out the cuff links now coated with grime and tossed them onto the desk, then the almanac chart that had gone stiff from the water. Shattner was very still in his chair now. "You'll find the missing link in all this when you track down a man named Richter," Sebastian said. "Bishop Hans Richter."

"He was at Johnny Vandermeer's apartment the same night Shattner propositioned me on the operation. You could try finding him at the Kaiser Wilhelm Church."

"General Kelland?" Shattner cut in sharply now, rising to his feet as if he wanted to end it all right there. "I have not denied that I had a meeting with Herr Udal at Herr Vandermeer's that night, right? It was there that I consented to let this man go through with his plan to smuggle out the documents, giving him the impression that I was with him. But there was no Bishop Richter there, on my word—all of this is becoming a bore to me and a waste of valuable time . . ."

Kelland said nothing and finally put the cuff links back down onto the desk in front of him. His voice was mild, unhurried. "Herr Udal, there is a verse of Scripture in Genesis 32:20 which says, 'Behold, thy servant Jacob is behind us.' Can you give me the context of that verse?"

"General, I protest—!" Shattner tried.

"If you please, Herr Shattner?" Kelland cut back. "This man is taking the risk, not you."

Sebastian knew it was now or never. Kelland was willing to make it a Biblical test, maybe the forte of Sebastian, the Achilles' heel of Udal. He closed his eyes against the burning pain of exhaustion, trying to rip off the paralyzing bind to his memory. "It would have to be Jacob returning from his flight from Laban," he finally said, staring at the floor between his feet. "I believe he is there returning to meet Esau; he sends his family and cattle over first, telling his herdsmen to tell Esau that Jacob is behind them." He paused, sensing that Kelland was waiting, that Shattner was ready to spring from his chair. "And after that Jacob wrestled with God and thereafter walked with a limp."

"General, you are making a fool of the Gehlen Bureau!" Shattner almost shouted it now. "You expect that to be proof that this man is not Kurt Udal?"

"Not at all," Kelland shot back, and his eyes were snapping gray-blue now. "But you know as well as I, Herr Shattner, that Kurt Udal was a lousy clergyman and a very poor Biblical scholar. You must know as I do that he flunked Bible history and Old Testament Survey twice in seminary and couldn't pass his oral exams before the Council two years ago that would have given him the Bishopric—"

"You are contradicting our information, General?" Shattner returned, his face now taking on a glow of pink in his anger.

"What I'm saying, Herr Shattner," Kelland returned

quietly, "is that this man could be Herr Udal in spite of that. But there is too much doubt about what has happened to this man in the last twenty-four hours to dismiss him as Kurt Udal, especially when the security of the wall is at stake. If his claim concerning Richter and the matching cuff link is true, then we have the responsibility to pursue it."

"And are you willing to take the responsibility of delaying our investigation about the documents, General?" Shattner bored in intensely now. "Bonn wants a report on this man—now, tonight! What if Udal has passed the documents already and they are in the wrong hands? Are you prepared—?"

"I am prepared, Herr Shattner," Kelland said finally and reached for his cap on the desk.

Shattner saw that he wasn't going to pin Kelland back. He stood there rocking on his heels a full minute, saying nothing, then said, "Then if you insist, I will be glad to look for this Richter at the Kaiser Wilhelm Church—"

"We will look together," Kelland returned and gave a quick smile. "Including this man here, Herr Udal or Sebastian, whichever he is . . . all right?"

Shattner shrugged and moved for the door, Kelland following, Sebastian coming last. Outside, Kelland asked Sebastian to put the name of his former church in Wisconsin on paper for a wire for confirmation. Sebastian put down the name of his old friend, Les Bennington, along with the church.

Then they went out. Shattner argued all the way, but Kelland said nothing. When they reached the familiar memorial, Kelland sent four of his men to cover the main exits. Then he took Sebastian and Shattner into the rear door of the main sanctuary.

The two ministers on duty remembered Richter, but he had left earlier in the day without saying where he was going. "He was here to install the carillon," one of them said. "And he's been playing it every evening for us for the last ten days or so . . ."

Sebastian figured it would be a dead end, except that at least Kelland knew now that there was such a man as Richter. There was nothing to do but go back to the office and start the search.

But Sebastian wasn't sure he was going to make it. He was dizzier than ever. Outside Kelland's office he wanted to warn him not to let Shattner out on his own, not to let him get to Willie Gurnt before he could talk.

But no words came. There was only Kelland trying to grab him as he fell, and Shattner's trace of a smile . . . then he blacked out.

He awoke with a start. Kelland's intent face was there beside the bed, swimming in and out of his drugged senses. Sebastian glanced at the clock on the side table—it read 8:30.

"Morning or evening and what day?" he croaked, sitting up. He still had the smell of the sewer on him, but he did not feel so exhausted now.

"It's eight-thirty P.M. Tuesday the seventh," Kelland said.

"That late?" Sebastian kicked his feet over the side of the bed opposite Kelland. By the looks of the room he was in, he was sure this was Kelland's special bedroom he used when staying in. "What about the Russian parade?"

"Slow down," Kelland cautioned him with a tired smile. "No Russian parade . . . too much trouble at the wall by you know who?" He paused a moment, then added, "Anyway, we found Richter."

"How?" And Sebastian felt a genuine relief now.

"At a castle in the Charlottenburg district . . . a Mr. Dorf Frantzel . . . I understand he visited you once there." Sebastian nodded. "Well, this Frantzel has been watching that castle night and day, still sure that you are Udal and still in the place. So he tries to find out last night, breaks in and gets caught by our MP patrol. That place is off limits except to Gehlen Bureau. When Frantzel insists he's looking for Udal there, that brings Western Intelligence into it and finally to us . . . we checked out the castle and found Richter hiding up in an attic . . ."

"The cuff links?"

"We have them—he was surprised when we demanded to see his. They're now down in decoding. There's microfilm under that quarter note as you suggested. So you've got it right so far. Shattner played the discovery straight since there's nothing to implicate him in all this—not yet."

"Is the pressure off me then?"

"As far as I'm concerned, yes. But we still don't have the proof that you are a double. Until we have proof, Shattner has a claim on you. With Frantzel still insisting you are Udal, I can't hold you against that."

"Time is running out," Sebastian insisted. "Has Willie come out of it? How about those kids in the balloons?"

"Nothing," Kelland cut in with a wave of his hand. "Gurnt is half in and half out of consciousness, not enough yet to talk."

Sebastian knew Kelland was worried by the way his big farmer hands gripped the back of the chair and the way he ran a hand through his short red hair, scratching his scalp. "You might as well come to the office with me," he said finally. "I'm bringing Shattner and Richter up in five minutes—maybe you could think of something while we wait for decoding."

Sebastian finished dressing and followed him out. On the way down the long hall to Kelland's office, he tried to think back to the last time he had met Richter in Johnny's apartment. His mind, cleansed of the sludge of exhaustion, seemed to open its memory bank for him, feeding out the stored images. He knew there wasn't much time to form theories. The next hour or less would be crucial to him, because Shattner would be desperate to get him out of the way.

Once inside Kelland's small but comfortable office, Sebastian decided to work on his one flimsy hunch. "Do you mind if I ask a blunt question?"

Kelland paused at the desk. "Shoot."

"That scar on your face . . . may I ask—?"

"Sure," Kelland said quickly. "A gasoline fire inside a tank in Korea. I got out, but it took a lot of plastic surgery at that. Some reason for asking?"

"You shy of fire now?"

Kelland shrugged. "Why should I be? You get over those things like a bad dream."

"Can we have a fire?" Sebastian said then, looking down into the empty fireplace.

"You cold?"

"No. Just a hunch I'm playing. It may not be a delicate way to prove my point, but I'm going to try."

Kelland built the fire in the fireplace, using dry pine twigs for tinder. A few minutes later the door opened and the two MPs came in, escorting Shattner and Richter into the room. "General, you realize that you are insulting the Gehlen Bureau by your actions here?" Shattner began in an outraged tone. Kelland didn't bother countering him. Sebastian looked at Richter. The same lined face with the peculiar orange-pinkish glow to the cheeks; the bushy flow of white hair, wild like a bramblebush; and the eyes greenish in their deep sockets. Sebastian was sure he saw the first signs of hate there.

"And my office called," Shattner was going on in a continual stream of invective, "and I had to tell them about Udal here. . . . They are coming to get him with a special escort. It will go hard on you, General, for their having to do that."

"May I invite you to sit down while you are waiting?" Kelland said politely, and indicated the chairs Sebastian had pulled up to the fire. Shattner seemed taken aback at this abrupt display of pleasantry. He blew his nose into his handkerchief in a snort of disdain.

"Bishop Richter?" Sebastian said, standing with his back to the fire and waving a hand to the cushioned straight-backed chair closest to the fire on his left. Shattner made a move for it deliberately, but Sebastian shook his head and added, "Herr Shattner, in Germany it is a custom to give the best chair to the guest in the city, yes?"

Shattner cleared his throat noisily and reluctantly took the chair on Sebastian's right, a few feet farther back than the one reserved for Richter. Richter looked very intently at Sebastian now. He accepted the chair as directed but immediately shoved it a few discreet feet from the flames, pressing hard against its back as if he were lifting his head and body from a bad smell. Sebastian watched him closely, looking for cracks in the poise of the man, waiting for the sign he had to have before he could try anything.

"There is no reason to hold Bishop Richter here," Shattner went on in his usual waspish tone. "There is no crime in a man carrying film in a cuff link . . ."

"Not yet," Kelland replied from behind the desk, his eyes watching Sebastian, as if he were waiting too.

Then Shattner struck a match on the bottom of his shoe to light his cigarette, and Richter jumped as though a bolt had struck a foot away. It was what Sebastian had waited for; he knew there had to be something in the flinch.

"—we would be interested in the microfilm, of course," Shattner went on, "but our concern is with Herr Udal here first."

"You cannot take this man until I have satisfied myself about the film Richter was carrying," Kelland snapped at Shattner. "And I'm still concerned about this man's identity—"

The buzzer on the desk intercom interrupted him, and he paused to flip the switch. "Gehlen Bureau escort outside, sir," the voice said loudly into the room.

"Tell them to stand by," Kelland replied.

"So," Shattner said with finality, turning to Sebastian and putting both hands on his knees in preparation for getting up, "it is time now, Herr Udal . . ."

Sebastian realized it was the end of the line then. If he was to do anything at all to check the pattern, he would have to risk the possible repercussions. But what did it matter now? If he failed in the attempt, he was no worse off. Richter was not the Kaiser after all, or hardly the Angel Gabriel. So he reached down and picked up an eighteen-inch-long pine branch, shoved it into the flames and waited for it to catch. "You'll permit me one indulgence," he said to Shattner, who was half out of his chair and sat down again on the end of it impatiently, elbows resting on his knees.

"General Kelland, I am not in the mood for any more of this delay," Shattner protested.

Kelland had come around the desk now. He stood in the open space between Richter and Shattner, his arms folded, watching as Sebastian lifted the flaming pine branch from the fireplace. The burning sap smelled hot and greasy. Sebastian moved a few steps forward until the flame was almost at Kelland's chest.

"Fire is known to have revolutionized man's environment, Herr Shattner; did you know that?" Sebastian said, and just then a loud pounding sounded at the door.

"General, I have people out there waiting!" Shattner warned, lifting up out of his chair again.

"Lock the door, sergeant," Kelland ordered, "and keep Herr Shattner in his chair!"

"General—" Shattner demanded again, his voice rising to a military command.

"So most people do not fear fire," Sebastian went on, lifting his voice above Shattner's, dominating the room now and everyone in it. "But General Kelland here has every reason to . . . a gasoline fire caught him in a tank and left him with something to remember a long time . . ." And Sebastian lifted the crackling yellow flame to Kelland's chin. Kelland did not flinch, but his eyes fixed on Sebastian through the fire and seemed to say, "You'd better be sure of what you're doing."

Sebastian moved on to Shattner, who had no choice but to sit there in his chair with the burly sergeant standing behind him. The pounding on the door was getting more insistent. Sebastian ignored it; so did Kelland. Shattner was desperate and his eyes narrowed as if he guessed what was coming; but he did not veer from the flame even as Sebastian said, "Herr Shattner has seen his share of fire, yes, perhaps much of which he started himself? But, you see, the controlled discipline allows for no fear . . ."

"General, you will regret this!" Shattner bellowed as the MP sergeant pulled him back into the chair.

Now Sebastian turned and moved toward Richter, whose bony hands were clenched in front of him, his arms resting on the wings of the chair. He was not moving. The face remained in its almost hypnotic trance; only the eyes dilated slowly as the flame spelled out its implications.

"The only people who really fear fire are those perhaps who carry on them flammable things; is that not right, Herr Richter?" Sebastian went on, moving the pine branch closer until it was only a foot from Richter, who had shoved his back so hard into the chair that it was tilting on its hind legs. "What has Bishop Richter to fear from fire then?" Sebastian asked above the pounding on the door. "What is it, Herr Richter, that you carry that is so sensitive to flame?"

"General Kelland!" Shattner yelled again, and he jumped up this time to try to fight the sergeant, who had to come around the chair to hold him. "You are disgracing a public servant! He is not yours to play with like this!"

"Well, what is he then, Shattner?" Kelland shot back. "He's a man carrying microfilm, hiding in one of your castles and unable to properly identify himself as a member of the National German Church! I have every right to test him, Herr Shattner—"

"Then do it under the protest of the Gehlen Bureau!" Shattner shouted back, trying to pull out of the sergeant's grasp to get at Sebastian.

But now Richter felt the chair tip too far back on him, and he jumped up and made a run for the door. One of the MPs blocked his way. He spun around then, putting himself up against the wall, hands extended out flat as if he were trying to keep the wall from falling on him.

"Shatt-n-e-r!" he bellowed, like a man being crushed in

the inventions of his own making. Sebastian followed him with the torch, conscious of Shattner's continued howling in the room, the urgent pounding on the door, the sputtering of his own heart, for he was closing in now, and he had to go all the way if he was to stay alive himself.

"Stop it!" Richter shouted in German then as the flame waved under his nose. The shout was strong, appealing, demanding—youthful. Not the high-pitched and wheezing stammer of that night in Johnny's apartment. And as Sebastian pushed the flame even closer, Richter lifted his head toward the ceiling in a straining motion to climb out of reach, while his hands flapped against the wall in clawing motions.

And then as the sounds seemed to mix in awful crescendo, and the room turned into a pressure cooker, it happened. Richter began to tear at his face, pulling strings of skin from his face—the bushy eyebrows came off with a jerk, then the lumps around the bridge of the nose, the strips of pencillike scratches on his cheeks. The pounding on the door had stopped and the room had gone still too, except for the popping grease in the flaming pine branch that poured a garish light over the macabre performance. "It will make no difference!" he shouted as he continued ripping off the make-up. "The code is already passed! The hour of destiny arrives!" and off came another chunk of the make-up from the heavy chin. "Soon the Communist menace will be ended! Soon the power of the Reichstag will rise to its glory again and deliver us!"

And then as a final, crowning point of his vituperation, he pulled off the huge mane of white bushy hair, and he stood there to let them absorb the effect. "Yes!" he snapped at them in crisp English, his gray-green eyes lighting in triumph, his lean carriage going stiff with pride. "The real Kurt Udal, General Kelland! The Esau that finally made a mouse of this Jacob—yes?"

Nobody said anything. Even Shattner was silent. Sebastian dropped the half-burned branch into the fire. "I don't know who made a mouse out of whom," Kelland said calmly, "but I know who found the rat here, Herr Udal!"

"General, I insist that you let my men into this room!" Shattner ordered, still trying to prevent dissolution of the perimeter he had commanded up to now.

"Herr Shattner, I am holding you and Herr Udal," Kelland said flatly, "until the Gehlen Bureau takes over."

"It won't change anything, you fool," Shattner replied acidly, his hat shoved back on his head now to reveal that single twig of sweaty gray-black hair in the open field of his bald spot; it was the first real sign of disarray Sebastian had seen in him. "That clumsy fool there," and he jerked his head toward Sebastian, "may have kicked over a few rocks, but we have done what we planned. In the end you will rise up and bless the memory of us. If you are what I think you are, General, you will not try to interfere now!"

But Kelland only looked at them as if they were mad, and said to the MPs, "Handcuff them and take them away . . . we'll talk later. Make sure they are under maximum security at all times."

"And how many rocks did Johnny Vandermeer kick over, Shattner?" Sebastian threw in then as the MPs put the handcuffs on them.

"Like yourself, his mixed loyalties got to him too soon," Shattner returned snidely. "He was with us all the way, don't forget that. He knows as a churchman—even as you should—that you cannot exist with Communism, yes? He believed in our cause! But then he decided suddenly he didn't want any part of touching a hair on your head—so he had to be removed . . ."

They turned to move out under the armed escort, and as they did so, Udal's eyes locked with Sebastian's for a minute. Sebastian sensed in that steady gaze both derision and a grudging kind of salute—it was really Jacob and Esau meeting across that river in a strange kind of reunion, two men of opposite character and conviction. Udal might have said something then, but as the MP touched his arm, he thought better of it and simply smiled a thin, lifeless grin and went out.

As they went out, the three men in uniform swept in.

"Was that you pounding out there, Heath?" Kelland asked.

"We were about to call the bloody bomb squad," Heath said. "We got the microfilm developed and ready—that's why we ran up here and made the fuss . . ."

Kelland introduced the three as Heath, Monteau and Bollweg and then got on the interoffice phone to instruct his aid to inform Crisler of the Gehlen Bureau that he was holding Shattner.

He hung up and said to his three assistants, "This man Sebastian blew the cover on Richter, who turned out to be Udal hiding under a clever make-up job. The cuff links he wore make sense now. Both he and Shattner are in it up to their necks—the question is what."

Nobody said anything, feeling perhaps as if they would have liked more details on how Sebastian broke it with Richter. Then Heath laid out the enlarged slides of the microfilm on Kelland's desk.

"We can't break the code yet," he said, and Sebastian moved over to look at the diagram. "One is nothing more than a sheet of music to the hymn 'A Mighty Fortress Is Our God'—but oddly enough one whole line has four quarter notes missing—"

"Well, the quarter notes make sense," Kelland added. "That's the fulcrum on which the whole operation rests, probably."

"Yes," Heath admitted, "but what's it supposed to mean? Is it meant to be played like that as a signal? And how do they play it and on what? And then there are five letters underneath—see there? G E L N D. We've tried unscrambling that—"

"Why not this?" Sebastian offered, and wrote on the blank pad beside the frame:

G—Genesis
E—Exodus

L—Leviticus
N—Numbers
D—Deuteronomy

They all looked up at him blankly, and he added, "The Five Books of Moses, gentlemen—the Pentateuch—I was told I was going after, but they gave me the idea it was the original manuscript."

"That's what Shattner said it was," Kelland agreed, "Code Name Five Books of Moses."

"So?" Monteau put in, shoving his glasses up on his forehead. "What do the Five Books of Moses have to do with four quarter notes missing in a hymn?"

"You tell me, Colonel," Kelland returned crisply, "you don't ask, all right? You people are the experts here. And you'd better come up with it fast, because it is now ten o'clock, and whatever this code is, we'll probably know the ugly side of it by midnight."

It took another hour and fifteen minutes to argue it, to cross check, to write out puzzles on reams of paper. They even called in an expert from Western Intelligence, a man named Payne, a key man in cryptography. But it was young Colonel Bollweg who broke it finally.

"Supposing those five letters representing the first letters in the Books of Moses were the first letters of actual streets that cross the wall?" he asked from where he was sitting, with his feet propped up on a small table.

Nobody said anything for a good ten seconds. Kelland kept rubbing the back of his neck, staring at Bollweg. He turned quickly then and pulled the map down from the case on the wall behind him.

"Where are the Russian divisions quartered?" he asked, peering up at the enlarged map of Berlin.

"They've been moving all over the bloody place," Heath commented wearily.

"But where are the main staging areas, the billet areas?" Kelland insisted, and his voice was sharp now.

"Gitschiner Strasse," Bollweg began, because this was

his particular responsibility in the command here. "Ebertstrasse, Leipziger Strasse, Neiderkirchnerstrasse, and Dresdener Strasse . . ."

Kelland put blue pins on each of the points and stepped back to look at how close they clustered around Potsdamer Platz, except for Dresdener Strasse. "That could be it, gentlemen," he said. "The Five Books of Moses have the first letters of the streets this crazy Reichstag crowd intends to hit tonight . . ."

"Are they mad?" Monteau said in awe, his eyes big as he peered at the pins.

"You could say that," Kelland replied. "They've decided that the best way to defeat Communism and a divided city is to start a war with them . . . so they hit those billeting areas where the Russians are quartered, trigger off the big blast and hope to wipe out Communism through NATO's superior nuclear arsenal . . . then in the power vacuum sweep the Reichstag into control . . ."

"Won't be a bloody citizen left after a war like that," Heath said sourly.

"What about the hymn with the four quarter notes?" Bollweg asked.

"It has to be the signal," Kelland went on. "It has to be . . . . Somehow it's been arranged through Udal, who probably got word earlier as to where the Russians would actually be billeted over there, that they would use the quarter note as the operational communications code, the quarter-moon as the day of action. Somehow they must intend to play that hymn with those notes dropped as a signal to go . . . maybe over the radio. . . . Max, alert the second and third battalions of the German Twenty-first Panzers. Have them set up military roadblocks on those streets at least one kilometer from the wall. Then get them checking every warehouse and possible staging area where a small army might be holed up."

"Do we call up the other divisions?" Bollweg asked.

Kelland hesitated, trying to see the pattern as it was emerging. "No," he said finally. "Too many troops up here would panic the Russians and get West Berlin in an uproar. . . . We'll have to trust to those German battalions."

Bollweg got up and left. Silence hung heavy in the room for a long time as Monteau and Heath thought about Kelland's decision, and then Monteau suggested, "It seems to me that if we don't play that hymn at all, that should stop the action altogether."

"I don't think so," Kelland countered. "You know how these operations work here—they had to anticipate that their key man might get caught before he could signal or play the hymn as intended. So, not to play it could only mean an alternative plan of action."

"So we have to play it straight just as it is without dropping a note," Heath added conclusively.

"Why bother?" Monteau insisted. "Just throw your armored divisions on the streets leading to the wall. That way any attempt is bound to be stopped."

"I don't want any kind of battle going on anywhere around the wall tonight," Kelland said emphatically. "Those Russians are nervous . . . even if one vehicle got through or one stray shell—well, we'd be in it . . ."

"Let's get back to that hymn then," Heath cut back quickly, for they all knew now that they were on the countdown. "Udal must have had a backup man ready to play it on the chance he got caught. He wouldn't tie the signal to himself, would he?"

"I doubt it," Kelland replied. "But what is he using to send the signal? Radio? TV? Sounds too obvious to me . . ."

"The carillon," Sebastian put in then. All three of them, their faces pinched in the mounting strain, turned to him quickly as if he'd never even been there all the time. "The carillon in the Kaiser Wilhelm Church—it was installed about the time Udal got here, and he's been practicing on it for ten days."

"Can a carillon carry far enough?" Monteau asked skeptically.

"I heard the bells almost two miles out the other day," Heath said. "Anyway, they've probably got one man who is now waiting for it, a man who knows his music. When he hears it without the quarter notes, he'll fire the flare, or whatever they're using."

"Okay, we'll have to go on that," Kelland said flatly then. By then Bollweg had come back into the room. "Colonel Bollweg, get ten men and go to the Kaiser Wilhelm Church and clear everybody out of there. Find out how the carillon is hooked up and wait for us there."

Again Bollweg nodded and left.

"You sure they are waiting till midnight?" Heath asked.

"If they find out we got Udal and Shattner they'll probably jump off without the signal," Kelland returned. "But since it is now eleven-thirty exactly, I would imagine they'll delay till midnight, just when the quarter-moon is at the zenith maybe. . . . Timing is a factor now; they all have to go at once, and the only way to be sure is to have the carillon pass the signal—at least, we hope it's the carillon."

"So who is going to play it?" Monteau said, bouncing the sticky question off the others.

They all looked at each other, then at Sebastian. Sebastian shook his head. "There must be somebody who can play the carillon," Kelland put to them.

"Somebody at the church?" Heath suggested.

"I wouldn't trust any of those clergymen now that Udal's been there all week," Monteau countered.

"It's not the best hour to convince anyone to come out at our request even," Kelland added, and there were pearls of sweat on his upper lip now.

"I think I have the man," Sebastian offered. Once more those eyes swung around to him, and he saw the almost desperate look in them. "Willie Gurnt."

"He's hanging by a thread," Heath contradicted with a sniff. "Do you expect him to play this on the nose, every note of it, when he can't even walk?"

"Major Heath, if it's a performance on a keyboard of any

216

kind, Willie Gurnt would crawl there dragging his plasma bottles with him," Sebastian replied categorically.

"Do tell," Heath said, raising his eyebrows in a manner that suggested he would have to be shown.

"If he's conscious enough, we've got to try it," Kelland said finally.

"Can you be so sure of all this?" Monteau chimed in with his own dubious note.

Kelland paused to look at him while pulling on his cap. "I'm not sure of anything right now, Colonel," he said bluntly. "We could be chasing a lot of smoke, nothing more. But I'd rather be grabbing at the long shots right now than standing around here when the roof falls in." He picked up the phone then and asked for the Army hospital. After talking a few minutes, he hung up and grabbed for his coat off the hook. "Gurnt is out of it and talking now. He won't play a full concerto, but he might do what our friend Sebastian here suggests. I'll leave word with my staff to call every keyboard artist in town and send them to the church just in case. Let's go!"

* 15 *
Joshua With the Horns

When they got to the hospital only a few blocks away, Gurnt was in isolation. The doctors argued about anyone's going in, but when Kelland insisted, they had to yield. Sebastian looked down into Gurnt's face, looking haggard against the pillow. As his eyes focused on Sebastian, he gave a weak kind of grin.

"Joshua with the horns," he said in a scraping voice. "What . . . what horns you want blown now?"

"Willie, listen to me," Sebastian said as Kelland went around the other side of the bed, edging a concerned nurse aside. "How would you like to give the biggest performance of your life—bigger than the Berlin Opera?"

Willie's eyes opened again, peering at Sebastian's face, trying to get the message. "I already did that, remember?" he replied, "How's—how's Fritz?"

"He made it out," Sebastian said. "That's all I can tell you right now . . ." He saw Kelland glance at him then as if to say he'd better hurry now. "Willie, I'm talking about playing on a keyboard . . . the thing you like to do the most . . . the thing you were born for . . ." Willie's eyes seemed to take on understanding then, and little pits of light showed up in the deep tunnels of his tired blue-green eyes. "Willie, you said once that there were no tracks of God in Berlin. Sometimes, though, God can't

218

make any tracks except with the shoes He's given to us . . . your shoes, Willie. . . . I need you—Berlin needs you—to play one performance that could save Europe, maybe mankind."

For a moment it appeared that Willie was going to go under again, but then his eyes opened, and this time they were wider, a sign that somewhere inside his battered body the remnants of his torn spirit were gathering.

"Do you . . . do you ever ask anyone . . . something simple?" he said. "Like . . . like maybe pass the salt . . . or tie your shoes . . . or—can you find my pants?" And he gave a half chuckle and coughed on the pain.

Sebastian turned to look for Willie's pants as the doctor protested to Kelland, "This man cannot be moved! He'll die!"

"What are his chances lying there then, doc?" Kelland shot back.

"Not much better, but at least he'll have more time—"

"All right, we don't have any time—me, you or anybody else in the human race, okay, doc? So this man gets a chance to do something for all of us. . . . Can you get an ambulance ready?"

The doctor looked stunned, but he went off to do as asked. Sebastian helped Willie up off the bed and to a sitting position. Then they threw a coat over his white hospital frock and put him into a wheelchair. Willie did his best to cooperate.

"How about adrenalin?" Kelland asked. The doctor shrugged but gave Willie a needle. They went down the hall then to the loading dock and the waiting ambulance. The clock showed ten minutes to twelve.

They drove wildly through the streets, the klaxon howling its warning, all of them jammed in around the prostrate Willie, including the doctor.

"Let's sing it for him," Sebastian told them. "Just to refresh his memory . . ."

So they sang "A Mighty Fortress Is Our God," following Sebastian's lead uncertainly, their voices blending in peculiar discordant sounds, which seemed hollow and tinny in the crowded ambulance, but came from people who were not embarrassed to sing it or shout it, for now it was their life, their future, their hope. And finally Willie, that boyish shaft of hair poking in his right eye, opened his tired eyes to them and smiled wanly, lifting his hand to them weakly and managing to say, "It is not *that* strange to me, gentlemen . . ."

And then they were there, screeching to a halt in front of Kaiser Wilhelm Church. They got Willie out, but Kelland didn't bother with the wheelchair—he picked Willie up in his arms with the swiftness and gentleness of a man rescuing his own baby. He walked up the steps and through the doors. There he was met by Bollweg.

"The office called and said they have a concert pianist from the German Opera Company," Bollweg said. "But he is a good five minutes from us yet."

"Too late," Kelland said shortly. "This is our boy," and he nodded down to Willie, who looked barely able to breathe, his face pale as his smock, but his eyes carrying a steady shine. "The carillon . . . ?"

Bollweg nodded to the front. "It works off the organ . . . the switch has been thrown. Does this man know anything—?"

"He'll catch on fast," Sebastian said from behind Kelland, who moved through the dimly lit sanctuary to the organ up front, where he put Willie down gently on the seat.

"It's up to you now," Kelland said to Sebastian. "If I knew German, I'd like to tell him a lot of things. But remember, he's got to hit all the notes."

Sebastian nodded and got up beside Willie, who sat staring at the organ keys, looking perplexed. "There isn't much time, Willie," Sebastian said, and his voice sounded tense in the quiet of the sanctuary. He was conscious of the others watching him. "Try the *Warsaw Concerto* just for practice . . . get the feel of it."

Willie hesitated, his long fingers shaking now with the

220

effort, trying to caress the keys, then slowly stroking them until he heard the faint sounds of the bells high overhead in the glass tower. And he went through the theme of the concerto, frowning as he did it, not sure of himself, his lips trembling, but with a childlike wonder on his face now as he picked up the music from the bells . . .

Then Sebastian felt Kelland's touch on his back and saw the look that said it was now or never. So Sebastian took Willie's hands gently off the keys and whispered, "Willie, now is the time. Now you must play 'A Mighty Fortress Is Our God.' As we sang it, remember?"

And Willie sat there a moment, looking at the keys, and everything seemed to stop, all sound, all movement— and then he reached out and began to play, his fingers feeling for the keys with some uncertainty at first. But, catching the flow of the score, his fingers began to move more confidently. And after a moment, Sebastian stepped down from the organ platform, because he knew he wasn't needed any more. For Willie had taken command, his body sometimes bending under the pain; and as he played, each note was carried far on the cold night air. Sebastian saw it like the rest of them. Willie was not playing for Sebastian or Kelland or Berlin even . . . he was playing his own concert. For it seemed he was beyond any of them, touching something else in those keys, something that brought from his tired face a strange kind of concentration, but at the same time a peculiar look of understanding. It was his hour, his moment of destiny perhaps, and he knew it. And those who watched him there looked on with a sense of awe as if they were seeing a vision, and it subdued them so that their faces were no longer hard and masculine but like those of children, as if the world to them were neither ugly nor on the brink of disaster. It was as if all time and movement had ceased, and only the bells spoke the message. And what it said through the shaky hands of a dying man were things that each of them could not comprehend in their beauty and simplicity . . . and in that moment they were all neutral, free of conflicting ideologies, of military loyalties or political ties. It was, then, seemingly a return to innocence.

And then it ended. But nobody moved, for the sounds were still speaking to them in the quiet chamber. Then, suddenly, Willie slumped, and Sebastian was up, grabbing him, and Kelland was there too . . . and they lowered him to the carpeted floor by the organ. Sebastian got down on his knees beside him, peering down into the face that was fast showing the drain of the life left in him. The doctor checked quickly with the stethoscope, then slowly stood up and shook his head. Willie's mouth was open as if he wanted to drink the air that seemed so scarce to him now. His eyes remained bright, feverish, the light coming on strong in its last attempt to show life.

"You think . . . you think it is all right, yes?" he whispered. His hand reached up to grasp Sebastian's lapel.

"Perfect, Willie," Sebastian said. "You never missed a note."

He coughed, and Sebastian took off his coat and made a pillow for Willie's head. "Every man has his loose domino, yes?" Willie went on, fighting against the time running out on him. Sebastian nodded. "We all have it. . . . Fräulein Schell too . . . she fights to save it . . . her way with Ulbricht . . . but she finds it can only be your way . . ." And Willie grinned, as if it were a revelation personally satisfying to him. "And Dettmann . . . tough as the Wehrmacht . . . but inside he is a boy who needs a man's hand to touch his head . . . yes?" And now his fingers tightened on Sebastian's shirt, and he grabbed what was left of life to get it out. "And me . . . never too far to get my nose cut off, yes? Somewhere inside me too there is that thing that rattles around like—like a bone in a box . . . then God finds it. . . . When I grab that balloon, what I would never do . . . and then I know . . . like Margot . . . I know then what it is to touch the heartbeat of someone . . . you understand?"

"I do, Willie," Sebastian said, wishing he could pour life back into the frail body.

Willie licked his dry lips once, then added, as the lights slowly went out in his eyes, "So . . . you don't feel so bad now, yes? Your Joshua, now he blows the horns . . . *auf Wiedersehen* . . ."

And he was gone, quietly and majestically as the bells he had stroked in the strange, mystifying night. And when Sebastian looked up, no one was there—Kelland and the others had left them alone. And he stayed there a long time, overwhelmed by his loss, seeing them all march by again . . . Margot, Dettmann, Johnny, an old man named Obenoff, Kubeksten . . . names to be forgotten under the relentless boot of history. They had become a part of him now, joined to him in this terrible bed of pain that was Berlin. Then slowly he removed his coat from under Willie's head and covered his face with it. It was done.

He was alone on the roof of the AACN building. The night had a fine drizzle to it. Someone was getting a car ready to take him to the airport. He stood there watching the lights poke the sky for miles up and down the length of the wall. He had slept two days under sedation. When he had awakened, Kelland had given him what facts he had: Fritz had a broken arm and Rolf a big lump on his head from the rough balloon landing near Hamburg; Paul had come down in Stuttgart and suffered a broken leg. Kubeksten and Hans had landed in Holland; Kelland was sure Kubeksten had planned it that way, since he had already rented a shop for his diamond-cutting business. Sebastian received the news with relief.

As to the planned invasion of the wall by Shattner and Udal, Kelland simply said, "Until we get the full report, I'll just say we caught them flat-footed in their staging areas. But not a minute too soon. It was a fantastic attempt, to say the least. They must have brought those tanks and armored cars into those old warehouses piece by piece and assembled them by themselves."

Kelland hadn't added anything more except that the funeral for those who had died at the wall would be held that afternoon. It was raining when they placed the coffins of Margot, Willie and one representing Dettmann in graves by the Potsdamer Platz wall. They had moved Johnny Vandermeer from his grave by Ida Siekmann, where, strangely enough, Shattner had buried him according to Sebastian's instructions.

It hadn't been much of a ceremony. An Army chaplain read the service while the crowds of people watched solemnly from under their black umbrellas. Then Sebastian laid a wreath on each grave, and it was Major General Kelland who pronounced the most fitting lines to those who had gone:

"It is daylight, the sun is shining.
And again, for you and me comes the time to say goodbye,
And your boat leaves port with the wind and waves—
But fond wishes from your country go with you.
White roses of Athens, they say come back soon.
White roses of Athens, they say, auf Wiedersehen!"

Now he was here collecting what last memories he could, feeling the pull of the city even yet, realizing afresh what Johnny Vandermeer had found here and why he had thrown himself so recklessly into the vortex of this suffering. Sebastian was sure now that he would never judge any man of God on the kind of action he chose to take to relieve pain. Johnny had run his crooked miles for the glory of God; so had he. All he had proved was that he could run—but maybe that was enough.

Kelland came up and stood alongside him. They said nothing to each other. Kelland was smoking a cigar, and through the corner of his eyes, Sebastian saw him take it out, stare at it as if it were a poor symbol of celebration, and throw it over the side. With his hands deep in the pockets of his trench coat, he said, "I wish I could tell you that playing that hymn was the thing that wrecked the

224

invasion plans of Shattner and Udal and the Reichstag Party. I wish I could be sure, I mean. Actually, we don't really know. Those German battalions found those staging areas sometime before twelve, but we can't be sure. . . . I wish I could, because maybe the death of Willie Gurnt might have been more meaningful . . ."

"It was meaningful to Willie, General," Sebastian said, looking up at the lights again. "He played that hymn as something he wanted to do, had to do, irrespective of what it was or was not supposed to mean to the future of Berlin. Nobody will know what Willie found in doing that—it's between him and God now . . ."

Kelland did not reply immediately. He cleared his throat several times and then went on with, "Well, you couldn't have made it without the girl—or Dettmann—"

"You don't have to put jelly over it, General," Sebastian cut in on him lightly. "Thanks for trying, but I don't need it."

"Well, all right, but there's one thing you ought to know, just in case you get to wondering about it when you're five thousand miles away from here," Kelland returned bluntly, almost embarrassed now at getting caught in his good intentions. "You know you both ran over a mine field? You say the girl knew her way through it, but I doubt it. The construction tracks are covered up by the Grepos every night. That's why the armored car chased you . . . they thought you had found a way through and they could go the same way. Only they didn't, but you did . . ." Kelland cleared his throat again and added, "We figure maybe that had to be charged to some kind of miracle people like you carry around—maybe?"

Sebastian looked quickly at him, but the General was staring up at the lights now intently, rocking back and forth on his heels. "I figured she was guessing," Sebastian said simply.

"Yes . . . well, she was gambling a hundred to one on getting through. But she took the lead anyway, probably figuring if she hit the mines she'd get it before you, and you could still go over."

"Reversed roles," Sebastian mumbled to himself, seeing that sprinting figure again flying ahead of him, so sure of her every step.

"How's that?"

"I should have been out front laying it out for her . . ."

"Yes, well, to tell the truth, I thought of that too," Kelland returned. "But all I can figure out is that you must have done a powerful lot of converting over there to get that kind of loyalty—wouldn't you say?"

"For the NATO record, General?" Sebastian said mildly.

Kelland smiled in the half-light and shrugged, not pursuing it. "Well," he said with a sigh, "one thing you can take with you, Pastor . . . you gave the Berliners over here the incident they need. Ulbricht can't see it, but every one of those lights jabbing the wall—all twenty-six miles of them hunting for balloons—is calling attention to it. Maybe it doesn't mean as much to you as the other thing, but one thing's sure, these people needed it. . . . You'll probably never know how much they really needed it . . ."

Kelland's voice trailed off in deep contemplation of what he had said. Sebastian looked up at the lights again as they criss-crossed the sky, and he felt a strange affection for Kelland just then. The dampness and chill inside him eased somewhat, and it was as if God had touched him in the dark.

"The car is ready, sir," an aide said from the shadows behind them. Sebastian turned and clutched Kelland's hand.

"Thank you, General."

Kelland seemed reluctant to let go and added, "Your former church sent the wire. It came yesterday morning from your man, Bennington; he apologized for the delay. Out of town. But he said he would fly here immediately if you needed him." Sebastian nodded and moved to the

226

door leading down from the roof. "By the way," Kelland called to him, "you got any good ecclesiastical stock I should invest in?"

Sebastian paused, looking back at the strong man silhouetted against the tracery of searchlights behind him. "People, General," he said finally. "People are still the most valuable commodity that God has in the universe . . ."

Then he picked up his bag and followed the driver downstairs and out to the waiting car. They drove through the wet streets while the windshield wipers performed their rhythmic task. The driver began to whistle softly, and Sebastian recognized the tune to *"Edelweiss."* A police wagon rushed by them in the direction of the wall, its blue light flashing, its horn blowing into the continuing night.

Epilogue

General Alex Byronovitch
Director Military Security
Central Headquarters, K.G.B.
Moscow

PRIORITY A—CLASSIFIED

You have asked for clarification of the Jacob and Esau operation and subsequent events which have embarrassed the Ulbricht regime here in East Berlin. I hasten to give you only those deductions we have been able to make here, which, though inadequate, are all we can put together at this time.

First, your earlier counterintelligence reports indicating that the Jacob and Esau operation would in effect be an attempt to smuggle out documents for the Reichstag Party in the West were accurate. We made our plans accordingly and, as you ordered, allowed that the man who replaced Kurt Udal should be left to run without too much interference from us, since he represented the smallest link in the chain. Your order originating from the Central Committee of October 22, which permitted the Reichstag invasion to occur at the wall, was, I must add, brilliant; the fact that such a move would indicate clear provocation by the West and allow us the proper rationale to invade West Berlin and crush the NATO forces was indisputable. We had, as you stated, "a moment unique in history."

Let me now state why the planned invasion did not come off as scheduled. Our intelligence reports indicate that when Shattner and Udal were picked up on the evening of the seventh, the microfilm was still on Udal— although he had passed copies on to his associates—and General Kelland's staff cracked the code an hour before midnight. I believe it was purely by accident that the German battalions discovered the staging areas.

Further, I am afraid we underestimated the "Jacob" who took Udal's place. I had assumed, from what limited knowledge I have had of this decadent type called Christian, that we were dealing with the same kind of man as Udal—a man whose religion was but a blind for other concerns, a man who put the matter of espionage and political loyalties ahead of the inconsequential matters of the church. I had assumed, likewise, from my first contact with this Jacob—this Sebastian—that he was clumsy in his work as a spy, too obvious in his attempts to step in for Udal, and ultimately I concluded that he was no more a threat to us than a fly in a horse barn. I did everything to convince him that we did not know about him, of course. The fact of the matter is that he outwitted us, but in ways that we could not have anticipated.

What it comes to is this: While we were doing our best to make sure Udal got out to make his contact with the Reichstag, we were not watching what was happening with Sebastian. Somehow in those first few days—before the attempted assassination of him by Shattner, which you predicted as well—he must have managed to indoctrinate people around him with whatever the bourgeois church has that attracts the weak and the blind. However, it is a puzzle to us how he managed to cast such a spell on Margot Schell, our number one supervisor of civilian classification on the Office of Internal Affairs. This girl has always been dedicated to the Party, and though I could not understand her denying to me that Sebastian was a double for Udal, she was always too smart to be drawn into any scheme that was a threat to the Communist State. How she allowed herself to be corrupted by this Sebastian, we will never know, for she was killed at the wall. As for Willie Gurnt, he was merely a courier for Shattner, living off the few marks he received, a kind of vagabond piano player.

It is impossible to believe that Sebastian accomplished what he did with only a girl, a piano player, an old circus clown and a few children. We are certain that he must have had help from others in the system—we are still trying to find out.

We have sent the American clergymen back to the West, but only after Major General Kelland promised over the phone to return Udal to us when he is finished with him. Our agent "Langley," who got knocked around some by this Gurnt during the Jubilee, and who came over on the bus with Sebastian as you suggested, is also quite convinced that this man had a powerful underground working for him that we don't know about.

Meanwhile, we arrested an old man named Obenoff, who was Udal's caretaker at his church, and sweat him for two days to make him talk. But I am sorry to say that all the old fool said before he died was this:

"And the light shineth in darkness; and the darkness comprehended it not."

It is, of course, a quotation from the Bible, but it makes no sense to us at this point.

Meanwhile, Crisler of the Gehlen Bureau has disavowed any knowledge of Shattner's double-dealings with regard to the wall. And knowing him as well as we do, it would be hard to conclude otherwise. But the propaganda we can use against him on this count will help keep his agents nervous for some time.

But I regret most of all that the invasion did not come to pass as you anticipated. But, again, we have not dealt with

230

a man like this Sebastian before, and it is our conclusion that he was probably the best-trained agent they had, very disciplined, well drilled, and combining qualities of persuasion and insight that we have not seen the likes of before. That Shattner would sacrifice a man of such quality is understandable only in the light of his ultimate goal of starting a war. And knowing that Shattner was acting for fanatic right-wing interests in the West, this also would explain his poor sense of priorites.

We are still trying to quiet things at the wall. But this may take some time, since there have been numerous incidents of East Berliners who think they too can fly over the wall. Meanwhile, I remain

Obediently yours,

Colonel Gregor Chekhov
Military Attaché
K.G.B.
East Berlin